Grammar
Practice Book

Grade 4

Harcourt
SCHOOL PUBLISHERS

www.harcourtschool.com

ISBN 10   0-15-349911-7
ISBN 13   978-0-15-3499111

1 2 3 4 5 6 7 8 9 10   073   12 11 10 09 08 07 06

Contents

Contents

Name _____

▶ **Rewrite each sentence, using capital letters and end marks.**

1. my sister went to camp yesterday

   _____

2. the house seems empty

   _____

3. even the dog misses her

   _____

4. i will write her a letter

   _____

5. she comes home in one week

   _____

▶ **If the words form a sentence, write *sentence*. If the words form a fragment, add words to make a complete sentence.**

6. I went swimming.

   _____

7. The water.

   _____

8. Early in the morning.

   _____

9. Happy that you.

   _____

10. The week passed quickly.

    _____

▶ **Label each sentence below as *declarative* or *interrogative*.**

1. Vincent has moved to a new city.

   _____

2. He likes riding his bike in the new neighborhood.

   _____

3. Who is the boy on the red bicycle?

   _____

4. How do you like your new school?

   _____

5. Vincent has made some new friends.

   _____

▶ **Rewrite the sentences below. Begin and end them correctly.**

6. what time is art class

   _____

7. she rides her bike to school

   _____

8. where is the bus stop

   _____

9. i really like my new friends

   _____

10. who wants pizza for dinner

   _____

▶ **Read this part of a student's rough draft. Then answer the questions that follow.**

> (1) i went to visit my grandparents over the summer. (2) I missed my friends a lot at first (3) Then I found out that there were many things to do for fun. (4) Hiking, biking, and gardening. (5) Do you know what happened. (6) I didn't want to when the visit was over leave.

1. Which sentence is missing an end mark?
   A Sentence 1
   B Sentence 2
   C Sentence 3
   D Sentence 4

2. Which sentence has an incorrect end mark?
   A Sentence 1
   B Sentence 3
   C Sentence 5
   D Sentence 6

3. Which sentence is not a complete thought?
   A Sentence 1
   B Sentence 3
   C Sentence 4
   D Sentence 6

4. Which sentence has no errors?
   A Sentence 1
   B Sentence 3
   C Sentence 5
   D Sentence 6

5. Which sentence has words that are not in the correct order?
   A Sentence 2
   B Sentence 3
   C Sentence 5
   D Sentence 6

6. Which sentence is not capitalized correctly?
   A Sentence 1
   B Sentence 3
   C Sentence 5
   D Sentence 6

3

▶ **Rewrite these sentences correctly. Put the words in an order that makes sense.**

1. a new friend I made.

   _____

2. meet did you the friend at camp?

   _____

3. birthday party her will be fun.

   _____

4. will a present her you give?

   _____

5. time is what the party?

   _____

▶ **Rewrite each sentence correctly. Then label it as *declarative* or *interrogative*.**

6. what is your favorite thing to do

   _____

7. my friends and I like to spend time together

   _____

8. sometimes we play games

   _____

9. do you want to play outside

   _____

10. sometimes we just sit and talk

   _____

Name _____

Imperative and
Exclamatory
Sentences;
Interjections
Lesson 2

▶ **Label each sentence as *imperative* or *exclamatory*.**

1. Meet at the track at seven o'clock. _____

2. Run around the track four times to warm up. _____

3. I cannot believe how fast she runs! _____

4. You must be very proud! _____

5. Take your positions for the race. _____

6. What an amazing event this is! _____

7. We had so much fun today! _____

8. Follow me to the car. _____

9. Take a nap when you get home. _____

▶ **Rewrite the sentences. Add the correct end marks.**

10. Help me find my running shoes

_____

11. How nervous I am about the race

_____

12. I am so happy that you won

_____

13. Give her a bottle of water

_____

14. How tired they must be

_____

15. What a big trophy it is

_____

Name _____

▶ **Rewrite these sentences with the correct punctuation.
Then label each sentence as *imperative* or *exclamatory*.**

1. I was so worried about trying out for the school play

   _____

2. Don't give up on your dreams

   _____

3. Work hard in order to succeed

   _____

4. Hey your audition was amazing

   _____

5. Always listen to good advice

   _____

▶ **Draw one line under each imperative sentence. Draw two lines under each
exclamatory sentence. Circle the interjections.**

6. Take your places on the stage quietly.

7. Smile at the audience when the curtain goes up.

8. Ouch, you stepped on my foot!

9. Stand still until it is your turn to dance.

10. How wonderful this dance recital is!

11. Wow, she jumps so high and turns so fast!

12. Listen to the music so you will know when to start.

13. Hey, that's a great! costume

14. Wow, she is so strong!

15. Take a walk to stretch your legs at intermission.

▶ **Read this part of a student's rough draft. Then answer the questions that follow.**

(1) The soccer player is running down the field. (2) How very happy he looks. (3) Hey, he kicked that ball so far! (4) He has scored the winning goal for his team. (5) Listen to his coach praise him. (6) Wow, what a wonderful day!

1. Which sentence should have an exclamation point?
   A Sentence 1
   B Sentence 2
   C Sentence 4
   D Sentence 5

2. Which sentence is an imperative sentence?
   A Sentence 2
   B Sentence 3
   C Sentence 5
   D Sentence 6

3. In which of these sentences is the punctuation NOT correct?
   A Sentence 2
   B Sentence 3
   C Sentence 4
   D Sentence 6

4. Which of these sentences has an interjection?
   A Sentence 2
   B Sentence 3
   C Sentence 4
   D Sentence 5

5. Which of these sentences is neither imperative nor exclamatory?
   A Sentence 1
   B Sentence 3
   C Sentence 5
   D Sentence 6

6. Which of these sentences is an exclamatory sentence?
   A Sentence 1
   B Sentence 4
   C Sentence 5
   D Sentence 6

Name _____

▶ **Rewrite these sentences with the correct punctuation.
Then label each sentence as *imperative* or *exclamatory*.**

1. Wait for me after school

   _____

2. Put your uniforms on

   _____

3. How excited I am about the game

   _____

4. Bring me the basketball

   _____

5. Wow you are a good player

   _____

6. Tell us the score

   _____

7. Hey that player can really jump

   _____

8. Listen to the crowd yell

   _____

▶ **Write an exclamatory sentence with an interjection. Then write an imperative
sentence.**

9. _____

10. _____

Grammar Practice Book
© Harcourt • Grade 4

Name _____

▶ **Write the subject of each sentence.**

1. Everyone goes to the park. _____

2. Paula puts on her jacket. _____

3. We skip down the sidewalk together. _____

4. Darryl rides his bike on the street. _____

5. My mother holds my sister's hand. _____

6. They cross the street at the corner. _____

7. The park is crowded. _____

8. The flowers smell sweet. _____

9. I pick daisies for my father. _____

10. The sky has big white clouds. _____

▶ **Write the predicate of each sentence.**

11. Some boys run past us. _____

12. A dog chases a ball. _____

13. Paula climbs up the slide. _____

14. My sister plays in the sand. _____

15. Darryl makes a new friend. _____

16. Everybody loves the park. _____

17. The children shout with excitement. _____

18. No one wants to go home. _____

19. The sun sets behind the hill. _____

20. This day will end soon. _____

Grammar Practice Book

▶ **Draw one line under the subject. Draw two lines under the predicate.**

1. I visit my grandparents.

2. Their house has a garden.

3. I help pull carrots.

4. My grandfather makes wonderful soup.

5. I set the table.

6. He puts flowers in a vase.

7. We eat dinner together.

8. Everyone is full.

9. My grandmother brings out a cake.

10. I am hungry again!

▶ **Add a subject or predicate as needed. Write the new sentence.**

11. The brown dog.

   _____

12. played cards together.

   _____

13. is high in the sky.

   _____

14. went to bed.

   _____

15. My grandmother.

   _____

Read this part of a student's rough draft. Then answer the questions that follow.

> (1) Today was the big parade. (2) The marching band moved quickly down the street. (3) The music was loud and joyful. (4) Saw someone on the sidewalk. (5) My friend. (6) I waved my flag at him.

1. Which two sentences are fragments?
   A   Sentences 1 and 2
   B   Sentences 1 and 5
   C   Sentences 2 and 4
   D   Sentences 4 and 5

2. Which sentence is missing a subject?
   A   Sentence 1
   B   Sentence 2
   C   Sentence 4
   D   Sentence 5

3. Which is NOT a subject in the passage?
   A   The marching band
   B   The music
   C   Saw
   D   I

4. Which sentence is missing a predicate?
   A   Sentence 1
   B   Sentence 2
   C   Sentence 4
   D   Sentence 5

5. Which word is the subject of Sentence 6?
   A   I
   B   waved
   C   flag
   D   him

6. Which is the predicate of Sentence 3?
   A   The music
   B   was loud
   C   and joyful
   D   was loud and joyful

Name _____

▶ **Underline each subject once. Underline each predicate twice.**

1. The summer is long and hot.

2. Everybody sits on the front steps.

3. No one wants to move.

4. We decide to make ice cream.

5. I find a recipe in a cookbook.

6. My parents help.

7. The ice cream is cold and delicious.

8. Everyone eats a big portion.

9. My family is happy.

10. The day feels much cooler.

▶ **Add a subject or a predicate to complete each sentence.**

11. The street party _____

12. _____ played music.

13. _____ danced fast.

14. The food _____

15. All the people _____

16. _____ had a great time.

Name _____

▶ **Draw a line under the complete subject. Circle the simple subject.**

1. San Francisco is a city in California.

2. A big earthquake rocked the city in 1906.

3. The ocean view is magnificent.

4. A nearby city is Oakland.

5. The average winter temperature is 55°F.

6. The biggest park is Golden Gate Park.

7. One neighborhood is called Chinatown.

▶ **Draw a line under the complete predicate. Circle the simple predicate.**

8. Golden Gate Park has several landmarks.

9. The park survived the earthquake of 1906.

10. It has a lake with an island.

11. Three dogs ran up the big hill in the park.

12. The old man waved to his wife.

13. A woman held a yellow kite.

14. A boy walked over one of the stone bridges.

15. A girl did cartwheels across the lawn.

Try This

Write three different sentences that use the complete predicate below. Include descriptive words in each subject.

dived into the water

Grammar Practice Book
© Harcourt • Grade 4

▶ **Add a complete subject to each predicate. Then circle
the simple subject.**

1. _____ waited patiently for hours.

2. _____ learned to play a new game.

3. _____ ate his lunch.

4. _____ wanted to see his father.

5. _____ felt worried.

6. _____ finally left the island.

7. _____ stood on the pier.

8. _____ waved happily.

9. _____ jumped up and down.

10. _____ flew over the water.

▶ **Add a complete predicate to each subject. Then circle the simple predicate.**

11. The ocean waves _____

12. The cold porridge _____

13. A beautiful plum tree _____

14. The huge room _____

15. The new teacher _____

16. The bright light of morning _____

17. A happy man _____

18. The excited child _____

▶ **Read this part of a student's rough draft. Then answer the questions that follow.**

> (1) My whole family went to the Asian Art Museum in San Francisco yesterday. (2) This amazing museum has more than 14,000 objects in its collection. (3) A helpful museum guide told us a lot about the art. (4) We saw bronze statues, ceramics, puppets, and baskets. (5) The tiny carvings were my favorite things.

1. Which is the simple subject of Sentence 3?

  A museum

  B guide

  C us

  D art

2. Which is the simple predicate of Sentence 2?

  A has

  B more

  C in

  D its

3. Which is the complete predicate of Sentence 3?

  A told us

  B about the art

  C told us a lot

  D told us a lot about the art

4. Which is the complete subject of Sentence 1?

  A My whole family

  B Asian Art Museum

  C San Francisco

  D yesterday

5. Which is the simple subject of Sentence 5?

  A tiny carvings

  B carvings

  C were

  D favorite

6. Which word is NOT part of the complete predicate of Sentence 4?

  A baskets

  B bronze

  C saw

  D We

Grammar Practice Book
© Harcourt • Grade 4

▶ Match the subjects and predicates in the box to write sentences. Then draw one line under each simple subject and two lines under each simple predicate.

The excited girl	blew the leaves in the trees.
The cool wind	ran down the hill together.
A small insect	were fun to climb.
Several friends	shouted to her friend.
Three big rocks	jumped onto the branch.

1. _____

2. _____

3. _____

4. _____

5. _____

▶ Add a complete subject or a complete predicate to complete each sentence.

6. _____ went to a concert in the park.

7. _____ played traditional Chinese harps.

8. _____ became very quiet.

9. The audience _____

10. The grateful musicians _____

► **Read this part of a student's rough draft. Then answer the questions that follow.**

(1) The band has just stopped playing. (2) Do you see the lead singer smiling? (3) How happy she looks. (4) Look at the guitar player waving to the crowd. (5) He told me that they are playing another concert tomorrow? (6) Wow, so great!

1. Which sentence is an interrogative sentence?
   A   Sentence 1
   B   Sentence 2
   C   Sentence 4
   D   Sentence 6

2. Which sentence is an imperative sentence?
   A   Sentence 2
   B   Sentence 3
   C   Sentence 4
   D   Sentence 5

3. Which sentence should have an exclamation point?
   A   Sentence 1
   B   Sentence 2
   C   Sentence 3
   D   Sentence 4

4. Which is not a complete sentence?
   A   Sentence 1
   B   Sentence 3
   C   Sentence 5
   D   Sentence 6

5. Which of these sentences is correct as it is?
   A   Sentence 2
   B   Sentence 3
   C   Sentence 5
   D   Sentence 6

6. Which sentence is a declarative sentence?
   A   Sentence 1
   B   Sentence 2
   C   Sentence 4
   D   Sentence 6

Grammar Practice Book

▶ **Read this part of a student's rough draft. Then answer
the questions that follow.**

> (1) My greatest dream is to become a playwright.
> (2) A playwright writes stories for the stage. (3) My favorite
> playwright is Lorraine Hansberry. (4) She wrote a play called
> *A Raisin in the Sun*. (5) The title is from a line in a poem.
> (6) Hope to write a play as good as that some day!

1. Which sentence is missing a subject?

   A   Sentence 1

   B   Sentence 3

   C   Sentence 5

   D   Sentence 6

2. Which is the simple predicate of
   Sentence 2?

   A   playwright

   B   writes

   C   stories

   D   stage

3. Which is the complete subject of
   Sentence 3?

   A   playwright

   B   My favorite playwright

   C   is Lorraine Hansberry

   D   Lorraine Hansberry

4. Which is the complete predicate of
   Sentence 4?

   A   She wrote

   B   She wrote a play

   C   a play called *A Raisin in the Sun*

   D   wrote a play called *A Raisin in
       the Sun*

5. Which is the simple subject of
   Sentence 5?

   A   title

   B   is

   C   line

   D   poem

6. Which word is NOT part of the
   complete subject of Sentence 1?

   A   dream

   B   greatest

   C   playwright

   D   My

Name _____

▶ **Label each sentence *compound subject* or *compound predicate*.**

1. The two girls cleared the table and washed the dishes.

   _____

2. Tyler and Amir raked leaves together.

   _____

3. Ms. Lopez finished baking and cleaned the kitchen.

   _____

4. My mother made the shelves and framed the painting.

   _____

5. Dora and Carlos helped their parents.

   _____

▶ **Rewrite each pair of sentences as one sentence with a compound subject or a compound predicate. Draw one line under each compound subject. Draw two lines under each compound predicate.**

6. Leah kicks the ball. Leah passes the ball.

   _____

7. The swim team laughs. The swim team cheers.

   _____

8. Jamie runs around the track. His brother runs around the track.

   _____

9. The teachers clap. The schoolchildren clap.

   _____

10. Petra watched the game. Petra took pictures.

    _____

Grammar Practice Book
© Harcourt • Grade 4

Name _____

▶ **Rewrite each group of sentences as one sentence with a
compound subject. Use *and* or *or*. Use commas as needed.**

1. Beatrice paints the fence. Her brother paints the fence. Her sister paints the fence.

   _____

2. Dean bakes bread on Saturday. His mother bakes bread on Saturday.

   _____

3. Chan takes out the trash. Sometimes her grandfather takes out the trash.

   _____

4. Paolo cleans the garage today. His uncle cleans the garage today. His cousin
   cleans the garage today.

   _____

5. The children sweep the attic. Their parents sweep the attic.

   _____

▶ **Rewrite each group of sentences as one sentence with a compound predicate.
Use *and* or *or*. Use commas as needed.**

6. We went to the store. We bought supplies for the camping trip.

   _____

7. Ana put up the tent. Ana collected sticks. Ana made a campfire.

   _____

8. The park rangers searched the woods. The park rangers looked for fallen trees.

   _____

9. You can put the wood by the tent. You can leave it near the tree.

   _____

10. Fiona walked by the creek. Fiona collected blackberries. Fiona ate them.

    _____

Grammar Practice Book

▶ **Read this part of a student's rough draft. Then answer the questions that follow.**

> (1) My sister, my cousin and I cleaned our grandparents' basement. (2) I recycled old newspapers and threw out trash. (3) My older sister and my cousin organized the gardening tools and sorted through old toys. (4) We worked hard all day. (5) Then my grandparents, my sister, my cousin, and I celebrated a job well done.

1. Which of these sentences does NOT have a compound subject?

   A   Sentence 1

   B   Sentence 3

   C   Sentence 4

   D   Sentence 5

2. Which sentence is missing a comma?

   A   Sentence 1

   B   Sentence 2

   C   Sentence 3

   D   Sentence 4

3. Which are the simple subjects of Sentence 3?

   A   *older* and *sister*

   B   *sister* and *cousin*

   C   *older* and *tools*

   D   *toys* and *cousin*

4. Which are the simple predicates of Sentence 3?

   A   *organized* and *sorted*

   B   *organized* and *gardening*

   C   *gardening* and *sorted*

   D   *sorted* and *through*

5. Which of these sentences has neither a compound subject nor a compound predicate?

   A   Sentence 2

   B   Sentence 3

   C   Sentence 4

   D   Sentence 5

6. Which sentence has both a compound subject and a compound predicate?

   A   Sentence 1

   B   Sentence 2

   C   Sentence 3

   D   Sentence 5

Name _____

▶ **Each sentence has a compound subject or a compound predicate. Circle the compound subject or the compound predicate.**

1. Maria collects the tickets and tears them in half.

2. Juan and Reid help people find their seats.

3. The musicians and their friends build the stage.

4. Quinton, Jules, and Simon are the lead singers.

5. Rhea or Kyle can help you find your costume.

6. We fit the costumes and pin up the hems.

7. The performers sing or dance.

▶ **Complete each sentence. Add a compound subject or a compound predicate as shown in parentheses ( ). Remember to add commas as needed.**

8. Jonah _____. (compound predicate)

9. _____ picked up rocks. (compound subject)

10. My dog _____. (compound predicate)

11. _____ started growing. (compound subject)

12. My father and my brother _____. (compound predicate)

Name _____

▶ **Label each sentence *simple* or *compound*.**

1. Jeremy washes and dries the dishes. _____

2. I set the table, or I make the toast. _____

3. Mother goes to the store, and Jeremy goes with her. _____

4. I thought breakfast was ready, but the bacon is still cooking. _____

5. The eggs and sausages are on the stove. _____

6. I pour the orange juice, and Jeremy serves it. _____

7. My favorite meal is breakfast. _____

8. Sometimes we have pancakes, but today we have waffles. _____

9. The syrup is in the brown jug. _____

10. The flowers look pretty in the center of the table. _____

▶ **Rewrite each pair of sentences as a compound sentence, using the conjunction in parentheses ( ).**

11. Shauna likes horses. She rides them every summer. (and)

_____

12. She says she won a riding trophy. I have never seen it. (but)

_____

13. I swim in the lake. I fish at the river. (or)

_____

14. Shauna and I go camping. I show her how to fish. (and)

_____

15. We catch several fish. We let them go. (but)

_____

Grammar Practice Book
© Harcourt • Grade 4

Name _____

▶ Identify each word group as a *comma splice* or *run-on sentence.* Then rewrite each one correctly as a compound sentence.

1. The ranch is large, I walk all the way around it.

_____

2. I help him with some of the chores he thanks me.

_____

3. We can go to see the cattle, we can explore the barn.

_____

4. I water the plants, she washes the windows.

_____

5. We feed the hens we do not feed the horses.

_____

▶ Write each pair of sentences as a compound sentence, using *or, and,* or *but.*

6. I make my bed. I wash and fold my clothes.

_____

7. My aunt and uncle cook dinner. We all eat together.

_____

8. We can have chicken and salad. We can have pork chops and green beans.

_____

9. My grandmother is a good cook. She does not like washing and drying the dishes.

_____

10. I eat all of my dinner. I eat some dessert.

_____

Grammar Practice Book
© Harcourt • Grade 4

▶ **Read this part of a student's rough draft. Then answer the questions that follow.**

> (1) A campfire is nice, and it keeps you warm on chilly nights. (2) Make the campfire small sit close to it for warmth. (3) You can use branches you find on the ground, you should not take branches from a tree. (4) You can burn paper. (5) Do not burn plastic. (6) To put out the fire, you can pour water over it you can dig it up and turn it over.

1. Which of these sentences is a run-on sentence?

   A Sentence 1

   B Sentence 2

   C Sentence 3

   D Sentence 4

2. To rewrite sentences 4 and 5 as a compound sentence, which do you need to add between the words *paper* and *do*?

   A a comma

   B a comma and the conjunction *and*

   C a comma and the conjunction *but*

   D Make no change.

3. Which of these sentences is a comma splice?

   A Sentence 1

   B Sentence 3

   C Sentence 5

   D Sentence 6

4. Which of these sentences needs a comma and the conjunction *or*?

   A Sentence 2

   B Sentence 3

   C Sentence 4

   D Sentence 6

5. Which is a compound sentence that is written correctly?

   A Sentence 1

   B Sentence 4

   C Sentence 5

   D Sentence 6

6. How can you correct Sentence 3?

   A take out the comma

   B add the conjunction *or*

   C add the conjunction *but*

   D add a comma

Grammar Practice Book
© Harcourt • Grade 4

Name _____

▶ **Rewrite the sentences, adding commas as needed.**

1. Lela runs across the grass but she stops at the creek.

   _____

2. She can wade in the water or she can lie on the grass.

   _____

3. Lela tries to catch a small fish but the fish gets away.

   _____

4. Lela walks home slowly and she sits on the porch.

   _____

▶ **Tell whether each sentence has a *compound subject,* has a *compound predicate,* or is a *compound sentence.* Then circle each conjunction.**

5. A man and a boy are cooking together. _____

6. The boy collects wood, and the man builds a fire. _____

7. They smile and laugh together. _____

8. The man cleans up, but the boy sits quietly. _____

9. The boy waters and feeds the horses. _____

10. The horses eat hay, or they eat grain. _____

11. The sun sets, but it is not cold. _____

12. The moon and the stars will be out soon. _____

26

▶ **Underline the prepositional phrase. Circle the object of the preposition.**

1. This center teaches computer skills to students.

2. Today's lesson is across the hall.

3. After the break, there will be a demonstration.

4. There are several workstations in the room.

5. You can share a computer with a classmate.

6. Read the instructions on the chalkboard.

▶ **Circle each prepositional phrase. Write each preposition and its object.**

7. Hugo and Mia work together on a report.

    _____

8. Mia suggests getting information from websites.

    _____

9. They visit a library near their school.

    _____

10. The power switch is behind the monitor.

    _____

11. Mia searches for information.

    _____

12. The students feel good about their work.

    _____

✎ **Try This**

Rewrite this sentence several times: *We searched the Internet.* Add a different prepositional phrase each time. How many different sentences can you make?

▶ **Rewrite the paragraph. Choose prepositions from the box to complete each sentence. Use each preposition only once.**

above	about	with	to	into
in	for	after	on	through

Yesterday, my sister and I went shopping **(1)** _____ our grandmother. Early **(2)** _____ the morning, we left the house. We drove **(3)** _____ the electronics store. My grandmother led us **(4)** _____ the store. **(5)** _____ a while, we found the computer section. There were sale signs **(6)** _____ our heads. My grandmother asked questions **(7)** _____ each computer. My sister and I practiced typing **(8)** _____ the keyboards. My grandmother bought a new computer **(9)** _____ our home!

_____

_____

_____

_____

_____

_____

_____

▶ **Complete each sentence with a prepositional phrase.**

10. We are using the computers _____.

11. I am sitting _____.

12. The librarian is _____.

13. I see my teacher _____.

▶ **Read this part of a student's rough draft. Then answer the questions that follow.**

> (1) My family lives on a farm. (2) Before we eat breakfast, we do many chores. (3) Sometimes I collect eggs from the chickens. (4) On other days, I help care for the horses. (5) I use a pitchfork and get hay from the hayloft. (6) I place the fresh hay in their stalls.

1. Which is the preposition in Sentence 3?
   A   Sometimes
   B   collect
   C   from
   D   There is no preposition.

2. Which is the object of the preposition in Sentence 5?
   A   I
   B   pitchfork
   C   hay
   D   hayloft

3. Which is the prepositional phrase in Sentence 1?
   A   My family
   B   lives on
   C   on a farm
   D   farm

4. Which sentence has two prepositional phrases?
   A   Sentence 1
   B   Sentence 2
   C   Sentence 4
   D   Sentence 5

5. Which is the preposition in Sentence 6?
   A   I
   B   place
   C   the
   D   in

6. Which is the object of the preposition in Sentence 6?
   A   fresh
   B   hay
   C   their
   D   stalls

Grammar Practice Book
© Harcourt • Grade 4

▶ **Write each prepositional phrase. Underline the
preposition and circle its object.**

1. There are many kinds of computer systems. _____

2. Some computer programs are used in office work. _____

3. Other programs create art with drawing tools. _____

4. Many people play games on computers. _____

5. Friends send photographs through e-mail. _____

6. We use computers for learning. _____

7. If you walk into a school, you will see many computers.

   _____

8. Computers are a good source of information. _____

▶ **Rewrite each sentence, using a preposition from the box to complete it.
Use each word only once.**

after	with	on	of

9. _____ a power failure, you may lose computer files.

   _____

10. It is best to save extra copies _____ your work.

    _____

11. You can print files _____ a printer.

    _____

12. You can also save data _____ a disk.

    _____

Name _____

▶ **Tell whether each group of words forms an *independent clause* or a *dependent clause*.**

1. My father used birch for basket frames _____

2. Before he collected the plants _____

3. Because my aunts liked willow plants _____

4. My mother started to work _____

5. When she finished her bundle of plants _____

6. Since the birch trees were far away _____

7. We drove in a car to find them _____

8. When her grandson learned to weave _____

▶ **Find the independent and dependent clauses in these sentences. Draw one line under each independent clause. Draw two lines under each dependent clause.**

9. After the instructor gave the directions, all of the students began weaving.

10. The instructor was pleased because the students worked quietly.

11. While the students practiced, the instructor walked around the room answering questions.

12. Because there were only ten sets of materials, two students shared.

13. Each person helped clean up, since this was the last class of the day.

14. When the class was over, the students thanked the teacher.

15. Before the students left, they showed their baskets.

🖉 **Try This**

Write a sentence about making baskets that contains one independent clause and one dependent clause. Draw one line under the independent clause. Draw two lines under the dependent clause.

31

▶ **Label each sentence** *simple, compound,* **or** *complex.*

1. My favorite material for weaving is pine. _____

2. Rita would show you her baskets, but she is too tired. _____

3. Before this year's festival, I will make many baskets. _____

4. After we finish this one, let's stop for the day. _____

5. There are so many types of baskets that I would like to make. _____

6. My friend and I asked for help in finding the right type of plants.

   _____

7. Eva made this basket, and I think it is so pretty. _____

8. I am happy that Paolo likes this basket, since it is my favorite.

   _____

▶ **Combine the pairs of sentences to make complex sentences. Use commas when they are needed. The connecting words in the box may help you.**

┌───┐
│   although   if   because   before   │
│   when   after   since   │
└───┘

9. Ms. Tamez goes to the mountains often. They are near her home.

   _____

10. Robert collects branches. Ms. Tamez looks for branches, too.

    _____

11. They found the plants they want. They walk home.

    _____

12. Robert and Ms. Tamez begin weaving. They eat dinner.

    _____

Grammar Practice Book
© Harcourt • Grade 4

▶ **Read this part of a student's rough draft. Then answer the questions that follow.**

(1) When Sonia wakes up in the morning, the first thing she does is go to her window. (2) Although she could listen to the radio she likes to check the weather by looking outside. (3) Sonia wakes her sisters, and she prepares a picnic lunch. (4) Since the weather is nice the girls will collect plants for weaving. (5) The basket festival is next month!

1. Which is an independent clause?
   A When Sonia wakes up in the morning (Sentence 1)
   B Although she could listen to the radio (Sentence 2)
   C she likes to check the weather by looking outside (Sentence 2)
   D Since the weather is nice (Sentence 4)

2. Where should there be a comma in Sentence 4?
   A after the word *since*
   B after the word *nice*
   C after the word *girls*
   D after the word *picnic*

3. Which is NOT a complex sentence?
   A Sentence 1
   B Sentence 2
   C Sentence 3
   D Sentence 4

4. Which is a simple sentence?
   A Sentence 1
   B Sentence 2
   C Sentence 4
   D Sentence 5

5. Which is a dependent clause?
   A the first thing she does is go to her window (Sentence 1)
   B Sonia wakes her sisters (Sentence 3)
   C she prepares a picnic lunch (Sentence 3)
   D Since the weather is nice (Sentence 4)

6. Which has a dependent clause that needs a comma?
   A Sentence 1
   B Sentence 2
   C Sentence 3
   D Sentence 5

▶ Rewrite each sentence. Add the type of clause shown in
parentheses. Remember to add commas as needed.

1. Although baskets are mostly used to hold things, _____

_____. (independent)

2. Before I use any materials for weaving, _____

_____. (independent)

3. _____ Maya collected
weaving materials in the mountains. (dependent)

4. _____ her mother
showed her how to weave. (dependent)

▶ Make complex sentences from the sentence pairs. Underline the independent
clause once and the dependent clause twice. The first one is done for you.

5. My school days end at 3:30 P.M. I help my family weave baskets.

When my school days end at 3:30 P.M., I help my family weave

baskets.

6. Artie wants to learn to weave. He can take free classes.

_____

7. My mother collects pine needles. She soaks them in water.

_____

8. Marian cuts many reeds. She will make baskets for the festival.

_____

9. Tonya finds a book about weaving. She tries to make a basket.

_____

10. The weavers sit down. They are ready to begin weaving.

_____

Read this part of a student's rough draft. Then answer the questions that follow.

> (1) My family cooks and eats dinner together. (2) We plan the week's menus on Saturday we go shopping for groceries on Sunday. (3) We make many different dishes. (4) My father and my sister like to make pizza, but my mother and I like spaghetti best. (5) I think making dinner is fun, but it is not as much fun as eating it!

1. Which sentence is a run-on sentence?

   A Sentence 1

   B Sentence 2

   C Sentence 4

   D Sentence 5

2. Which are the simple predicates of Sentence 1?

   A *My* and *family*

   B *family* and *cooks*

   C *cooks* and *eats*

   D *eats* and *dinner*

3. Which of these sentences is a simple sentence?

   A Sentence 2

   B Sentence 3

   C Sentence 4

   D Sentence 5

4. Which sentence has a compound subject AND is a compound sentence?

   A Sentence 1

   B Sentence 3

   C Sentence 4

   D Sentence 5

5. Which describes Sentence 5?

   A compound sentence

   B simple sentence

   C compound subject

   D compound predicate

6. Which is the subject of both parts of Sentence 2?

   A groceries

   B Saturday

   C menus

   D We

▶ **Read this part of a student's rough draft. Then answer the questions that follow.**

(1) Aunt Millie stood on the dock by her sail boat. (2) She suggested a trip across the lake. (3) Although I was nervous I agreed. (4) Before we could leave, we had to get everything ready. (5) After we prepared the boat, we sailed into the deep waters. (6) Because it was a great trip, I learned to love sailing!

1. Which of these is NOT a dependent clause?

   A Although I was nervous

   B Before we could leave

   C I learned to love sailing!

   D Because it was a great trip

2. Which is the preposition in Sentence 2?

   A she

   B suggested

   C a

   D across

3. Which is the object of the preposition in Sentence 5?

   A we

   B boat

   C sailed

   D waters

4. Which sentence has two prepositional phrases?

   A Sentence 1

   B Sentence 2

   C Sentence 3

   D Sentence 4

5. Which of these sentences is NOT a complex sentence?

   A Sentence 2

   B Sentence 4

   C Sentence 5

   D Sentence 6

6. Which sentence has a dependent clause that is missing a comma?

   A Sentence 1

   B Sentence 3

   C Sentence 5

   D Sentence 6

Name _____

▶ Write *common* or *proper* to identify each underlined noun.

1. The insect rests on the branch. _____

2. Thea takes a walk in the woods. _____

3. The tree is very tall. _____

4. My mother is in the garden. _____

5. Grandpa picks flowers. _____

6. The children see butterflies in the field. _____

7. The worm crawls along the ground. _____

8. Darron searches for frogs by the creek. _____

9. There is a picnic by the lake on Labor Day. _____

▶ Rewrite each sentence. Underline the common nouns. Circle the proper nouns.

10. My class celebrates Earth Day.

_____

11. We learn about many different animials.

_____

12. Our teacher is Mrs. Abrams.

_____

13. She talks about pandas and gorillas.

_____

14. Marie asks a question.

_____

15. On Friday we write reports.

_____

Grammar Practice Book

Name _____

▶ **Write the abbreviation for each of the following words.**

1. February   _____

2. Thursday   _____

3. Avenue   _____

4. ounces   _____

5. August   _____

6. miles   _____

7. Street   _____

▶ **Rewrite the words below. Replace each abbreviation with the full word.**

8. Dr. Vilar

_____

9. Henderson Rd.

_____

10. Mt. Mitchell

_____

11. 20 cm

_____

12. Mr. McDonald

_____

13. Oct. 23

_____

14. Tues.

_____

15. Mrs. Pilmar

_____

Grammar Practice Book
© Harcourt • Grade 4

▶ Read this part of a student's rough draft. Then
answer the questions that follow.

> (1) In the winter many butterflies migrate to mexico. (2) Millions of Butterflies fly across the United States. (3) My friend Jeremiah lives in Texas. (4) He counts the monarchs he sees migrating. (5) On September 12, jeremiah counts more than 100 butterflies in one hour!

1. Which word in Sentence 1 should be capitalized?

   A winter

   B many

   C butterflies

   D mexico

4. Which word in Sentence 2 should NOT be capitalized?

   A Millions

   B Butterflies

   C United

   D States

2. Which is the correct abbreviation for *United States* in Sentence 2?

   A Un.St.

   B US

   C US.

   D U.S.

5. Which is the correct abbreviation for the word *September* in Sentence 5?

   A Sep.

   B Spt.

   C Sept.

   D Septem.

3. Which word is a common noun in Sentence 3?

   A friend

   B Jeremiah

   C lives

   D Texas

6. Which word in Sentence 5 should be capitalized?

   A counted

   B jeremiah

   C butterflies

   D hour

▶ **Fill in each blank with a common noun.**

1. At the _____, we learned about ocean animals.

2. The tour guide showed us a model of a _____.

3. We also saw a film about _____.

4. Learning about the _____ was my favorite part.

5. Our _____, Ms. Rodondo, told us to get on the bus.

6. When we got back to _____, we wrote reports.

7. I told my _____ about my field trip.

▶ **Fill in each blank with a proper noun. Use abbreviations for titles of people.**

8. _____ is a park ranger.

9. We go swimming in the _____.

10. The park is closed on _____.

11. Tara and _____ like to collect rocks.

12. My dog, _____, barks at the birds.

13. Around the campfire, we sing a song called _____.

14. _____ drives me home.

15. On _____, I write about our visit to the park.

Grammar Practice Book
© Harcourt • Grade 4

▶ **Draw a line under each noun. Write an *S* for each singular noun and a *P* for each plural noun.**

1. The trip to the mountains was fun. _____

2. The visitors came from around the world. _____

3. My friend collected rocks. _____

4. The smallest stones were found by the stream. _____

5. There were rare gems at the museum. _____

6. The most valuable ones were displayed in cases. _____

7. The guide said that rocks are made of minerals. _____

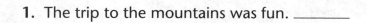

▶ **Rewrite each sentence. Complete each one with the plural form of the word in parentheses ( ).**

8. The scientists found _____. (fossil)

   _____

9. They heard _____ erupt. (volcano)

   _____

10. The damage was caused by _____. (earthquake)

    _____

11. The _____ were buried under ash. (city)

    _____

12. We enjoyed our geology _____. (class)

    _____

Grammar Practice Book
© Harcourt • Grade 4

Name _____

▶ **Write the plural form of each noun.**

1. person _____

2. man _____

3. woman _____

4. life _____

5. shelf _____

6. leaf _____

7. moose _____

8. fish _____

9. goose _____

10. deer _____

▶ **Rewrite each sentence. Replace the underlined word with the plural form of the noun.**

11. The <u>child</u> and the guide hiked up the hill.

_____

12. The rocks were sharp under their <u>foot</u>.

_____

13. They saw <u>mouse</u> run across the ground.

_____

14. One tree had marks from a bear's <u>tooth</u>.

_____

15. The campers had packed their <u>knife</u> for cooking.

_____

▶ Read this part of a student's rough draft. Then answer the questions that follow.

> (1) I live in a big city. (2) When I want to play outdoors, I go to one of the park. (3) At the park, I can play with other child. (4) I can see fish in the ponds, berries on the bushes, and birds and butterflies in the air. (5) Sometimes I play hide-and-seek among the tree. (6) I can do activities at the park for fun.

1. Which is the correct plural form of the word *city*?

   A citys

   B cities

   C cites

   D cityes

2. Which is the correct plural form of the underlined word in Sentence 2?

   A parkes

   B parx

   C parks

   D park

3. Which is the correct plural form of the underlined word in Sentence 3?

   A children

   B childs

   C childes

   D childies

4. How many plural nouns are in Sentence 4?

   A three

   B four

   C five

   D six

5. Which word in Sentence 5 should be a plural noun?

   A Sometimes

   B play

   C hide-and-seek

   D tree

6. Which is the singular form of the plural noun *activities* in Sentence 6?

   A activiti

   B activitie

   C activity

   D activitey

Grammar Practice Book
© Harcourt • Grade 4

▶ **Rewrite each sentence. Complete it with the plural form of the word in parentheses ( ).**

1. Did you see the wild _____ on the island? (pony)

   _____

2. We saw blueberry _____ on that hill. (bush)

   _____

3. The _____ ran through the forest. (fox)

   _____

▶ **Rewrite the paragraph. Change the underlined singular nouns to plural nouns.**

> Last week, I toured the (4) farm outside of town. At the first farm, I saw (5) pig, (6) horse, and (7) cow. Some of the cows had recently had (8) baby. Young cows are called (9) calf. The (10) owner of the farm told me many interesting (11) story about life on a farm. They also told me about some of the (12) job they do. One job is to feed the (13) animal. Another job is to shear the (14) sheep and the (15) lamb. I enjoyed my visit very much.

_____

_____

_____

_____

_____

_____

_____

Grammar Practice Book

Name _____

▶ **Rewrite each phrase, using a possessive noun.**

1. the paddle of the boy _____

2. the water of the campers _____

3. the canoe belonging to my aunt _____

4. the leaves of the trees _____

5. the nest of the birds _____

6. the cabin belonging to my grandfather _____

7. the backpack of my sister _____

8. the dog of the girls _____

9. the hose of the firefighter _____

▶ **Rewrite each sentence, using the possessive form of the noun in parentheses ( ).**

10. My _____ tent is red and blue. (uncle)

   _____

11. The _____ camping trip is a great success. (family)

   _____

12. The boy heard the _____ barks. (dogs)

   _____

13. Aunt Meg takes the _____ boots to the shed. (boys)

   _____

14. The _____ camp is down the hill. (women)

   _____

15. The _____ concern is that the bridge is not safe. (park rangers)

   _____

Grammar Practice Book
© Harcourt • Grade 4

Name _____

► **Identify each underlined noun as *plural*, *singular possessive*, or *plural possessive*.**

1. At the <u>park's</u> entrance, there is an information booth. _____

2. The <u>booth's</u> sign asks visitors to be careful. _____

3. It is <u>visitors'</u> responsibility to prevent forest fires. _____

4. <u>Matches</u> are used to light a campfire. _____

5. Sometimes <u>fires'</u> flames do not go out immediately. _____

6. When the fire is out, pour water over the <u>ashes</u>. _____

7. Dry <u>grasses</u> catch fire quickly. _____

8. A <u>tree's</u> leaves can burn, too. _____

9. Firefighters watch the forest from tall lookout <u>towers</u>. _____

10. A <u>firefighter's</u> tools for fighting fires include hoses. _____

► **Write the plural, singular possessive, and plural possessive form of each noun.**

11. moose _____

12. calf _____

13. goose _____

14. wolf _____

15. knife _____

16. community _____

17. dish _____

18. song _____

19. glove _____

20. table _____

46

Grammar Practice Book

▶ **Read this part of a student's rough draft. Then answer the questions that follow.**

> (1) Last summer, my friend's and I went to an orchard to pick apples. (2) The orchard's owners gave us baskets and showed us the rows of apple trees. (3) The apples' scent was sweet. (4) On each tree's trunk there was a ladder. (5) My friends and I climbed up the ladders' rungs until we were hidden in the trees' leaves. (6) We picked apples until our baskets were full.

1. Which word in Sentence 2 is a singular possessive noun?

   A   orchard's

   B   owners

   C   baskets

   D   rows

2. In which sentence is the word *tree* written as a plural possessive noun?

   A   Sentence 1

   B   Sentence 2

   C   Sentence 4

   D   Sentence 5

3. Which form of the word *apple* is NOT in the passage?

   A   singular

   B   singular possessive

   C   plural

   D   plural possessive

4. Which describes the word *ladders'* in Sentence 5?

   A   singular noun

   B   singular possessive noun

   C   plural noun

   D   plural possessive noun

5. Which sentence contains a possessive noun that should be written as a plural noun?

   A   Sentence 1

   B   Sentence 2

   C   Sentence 3

   D   Sentence 4

6. Which describes the word *baskets* in Sentence 6?

   A   singular noun

   B   singular possessive noun

   C   plural noun

   D   plural possessive noun

47

▶ Identify each underlined noun as *plural, singular possessive*, or *plural possessive*.

1. The boys' trip down the river was exciting. _____

2. I put the children's names on their backpacks. _____

3. The kayak's paddle was missing. _____

4. There were two seats in the large kayak. _____

5. The instructor told them to grab the paddle's handle. _____

6. The rushing sounds of running water got louder. _____

7. They fastened their lifejackets' straps tightly. _____

▶ Rewrite each sentence, using the possessive form of the noun in parentheses ( ).

8. The _____ favorite acitivity is to hike the trails near the school. (students)

_____

9. Adina knows which of the _____ signs to follow. (trail)

_____

10. Her _____ wish is to become a park ranger. (life)

_____

11. Using the map, we can find the _____ location. (campsite)

_____

12. I hold onto the _____ handrail as I cross the river. (bridge)

_____

▶ **Underline the pronouns. Circle each pronoun's antecedent.**

1. The farmer was happy when she got home.

2. Beth led the cow into her stall.

3. The man knew he had to buy more seeds.

4. When the trees grew tall, they shaded the house.

5. The horses saw the hay and began eating it.

6. Mr. Smith picked up the tools and put them in the shed.

7. Ms. Daniels has boots, but they are too small.

▶ **Rewrite each sentence. Replace the underlined word or words with pronouns.**

8. The cat picked up the kittens and carried the kittens.

   _____

9. The jar of peaches fell, but the jar of peaches did not break.

   _____

10. William asked Janine if Janine would rake the lawn.

   _____

11. The vet asked the owners if the owners had any questions.

   _____

12. When the boy saw the horse, the boy was happy.

   _____

Try This

Write two sentences using pronouns. Trade sentences with a friend, and rewrite his or her sentences, replacing the pronouns with nouns.

Grammar Practice Book
© Harcourt • Grade 4

▶ **Circle the correct pronoun in parentheses ( ).**

1. The farmers planted seeds. Then the birds ate (it, them).

2. Suddenly the rain began. People said that (it, he) would ruin the crops.

3. Nancy and Pablo hugged the dog. (We, They) told the dog to be good.

4. Please put the wheat in the barn. (It, He) will get wet.

5. Tom and Gwen were happy. (She, They) had grown a prize pumpkin.

6. Daniel was tired. (He, They) decided not to do his chores.

7. A calf was born last week. (They, It) weighed about 50 pounds.

▶ **Rewrite the following paragraph, replacing the underlined word or words
with a pronoun.**

> Jason, I want to tell (8) Jason about my trip to the mountains. (9) The trip was fantastic! I went with my sister, Dionne, and (10) Dionne had a good time, too. (11) Dionne and I went to the Rocky Mountains. (12) The Rocky Mountains were so beautiful! Although the temperature was warm, there was snow on (13) the Rocky Mountains. I made snowballs and threw (14) the snowballs at Dionne. (15) Dionne laughed, and (16) Dionne started throwing snowballs, too. Can (17) Jason believe that (18) Dionne and I had a snowball fight in June?

_____

_____

_____

_____

_____

_____

_____

▶ **Read this part of a student's rough draft. Then answer the questions that follow.**

> (1) Last spring, I met my friends Lydia and Gene. (2) They moved here from Texas. (3) Lydia, Gene, and I met at the creek by the school. (4) I liked to go there to listen to the water as it ran over the rocks. (5) Lydia and Gene liked to hear them, too. (6) Soon we were playing together every day!

1. Which word in Sentence 1 is a pronoun?

A Last

B I

C friends

D Gene

2. Which is the antecedent for the pronoun *they* in Sentence 2?

A spring

B I

C Lydia and Gene

D Texas

3. Which pronoun is used incorrectly in the passage?

A They

B I

C it

D them

4. Which pronoun could replace the underlined words in Sentence 3?

A They

B She

C We

D Us

5. Which word is the antecedent for the pronoun *it* in Sentence 4?

A I

B there

C water

D rocks

6. Which pronoun could replace the underlined words in Sentence 5?

A They

B We

C You

D Them

▶ **Underline each noun. Rewrite each sentence, replacing each noun with a pronoun.**

1. Tina brushed the horse. _____

2. Did Carter see Helen? _____

3. Mr. Finn found the rake. _____

4. The dog shook the bone. _____

5. Aunt Mary went with the girls. _____

6. The brothers waved to Mr. Lewis. _____

▶ **Write each pronoun and its antecedent.**

7. Dana and Giles told Lisa that she had missed riding practice. They walked her home.

   _____

8. After Phyllis saw the horse competition, she couldn't stop talking about it. She said it was very exciting!

   _____

9. Blake let Jasmin borrow the camera for the State Fair. She accidentally broke it. He was not angry, because it was old.

   _____

10. Jen told Grandma and Grandpa that they make the best apple pies. They said the pies taste good to them, too.

    _____

    _____

▶ **Read this part of a student's rough draft. Then answer the questions that follow.**

> (1) <u>Mistress</u> Hernandez, the camp swimming Instructor, announced some special events for <u>child</u> this Fourth of July. (2) There will be diving competitions, swimming races, and boat races in dogwood lake. (3) There will be prizes for all the winners of the events. (4) In the evening, a band will perform.

1. Which word in Sentence 1 should NOT be capitalized?

   A Mistress

   B Instructor

   C Fourth

   D July

2. How should the underlined noun in Sentence 1 be written?

   A childs

   B childies

   C childes

   D children

3. Which of these is the correct abbreviaton for the underlined word in Sentence 1?

   A Mr.

   B Ms.

   C Mrs.

   D Miss

4. Which words in Sentence 2 should be capitalized?

   A diving competitions

   B swimming races

   C boat races

   D dogwood lake

5. How many plural nouns are in Sentence 3?

   A two

   B three

   C four

   D none

6. Which sentence has no plural nouns?

   A Sentence 1

   B Sentence 2

   C Sentence 3

   D Sentence 4

▶ **Read this part of a student's rough draft. Then answer the questions that follow.**

> (1) My cousins', Jen and Angel, competed in a swim meet last week. (2) My brother Pablo and I like to watch them swim, so we went to the meet, too. (3) When Pablo and I arrived, Jen and Angel told us that they have lucky swimsuits. (4) My cousins must be right because they each won an event! (5) I got to hold my cousins' trophies and celebrate with them.

1. Which is the antecedent for the pronoun *they* in Sentence 3?
   A Jen and Angel
   B Pablo and I
   C brother Pablo
   D cousins

2. Which is the antecedent for the pronoun *we* in Sentence 2?
   A Jen and Angel
   B brother Pablo
   C Pablo and I
   D them

3. Which describes the word *cousins'* in Sentence 5?
   A singular noun
   B singular possessive noun
   C plural noun
   D plural possessive noun

4. Which sentence has a plural possessive noun that should be a plural noun?
   A Sentence 1
   B Sentence 3
   C Sentence 4
   D Sentence 5

5. Which describes the word *trophies* in Sentence 5?
   A singular noun
   B singular possessive noun
   C plural noun
   D plural possessive noun

6. How many pronouns are in Sentence 3?
   A one
   B two
   C three
   D four

 **Write** *SP* **for** *subject pronoun* **or** *OP* **for** *object pronoun*
to identify each underlined word.

1. Rebecca gave <u>him</u> a book about inventors. _____

2. Kyle asked <u>us</u> to help design a racing sled. _____

3. <u>We</u> were excited about helping invent a new toy! _____

4. <u>They</u> tested the racing sled on the hill. _____

5. <u>It</u> worked really well! _____

6. Kyle was proud of <u>it</u>. _____

7. <u>They</u> looked cold and tired. _____

8. Rebecca invited <u>them</u> inside for milk and cookies. _____

9. <u>She</u> said that chocolate chip cookies were her favorite snack. _____

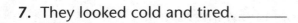 **Rewrite each sentence. Replace the underlined word or words with a pronoun.**

10. The fire escape was invented by <u>Anna Connelly</u>.

_____

11. <u>Drake and Claude</u> developed a new type of backpack.

_____

12. Maria Beasley designed <u>the first life raft</u>.

_____

13. <u>Eli Whitney</u> created many useful things.

_____

14. Would <u>these inventions</u> win prizes?

_____

15. The decision was not up to <u>you and me</u>.

_____

► **Rewrite each sentence. Choose the correct words in parentheses ( ).**

1. (Tim, Lisa, and I/I, Tim, and Lisa) are making a presentation.

   _____

2. Our teacher asked (Tim and me/me and Tim) to do some research.

   _____

3. Then (I and Lisa/Lisa and I) worked on the next part.

   _____

4. (I and she/She and I) drew pictures of famous inventions.

   _____

5. Tim read his introduction to (me and Lisa/Lisa and me).

   _____

6. Our teacher congratulated (Tim, Lisa, and me/me, Tim, and Lisa).

   _____

► **If the order of pronouns in the sentence is correct, write *correct*. If the order is incorrect, rewrite the sentence correctly.**

7. I and Lana read a book about Sarah Goode.

   _____

8. She and I studied women inventors.

   _____

9. I and you must decide which book to read next.

   _____

10. Heather invited Dominic and me to study with her.

   _____

▶ **Read this part of a student's rough draft. Then answer the questions that follow.**

> (1) Today me and Ella learned about an inventor named Sarah Goode. (2) Have you heard of Sarah Goode? (3) In the 1880s, she saw that families living in cities had very small apartments, and families needed to save space. (4) Her designed a new kind of bed. (5) _____ folded into a cabinet and became a desk. (6) I think that invention is clever!

1. Which words should replace the words *me and Ella* to correct Sentence 1?

   A   Ella and me

   B   Ella and I

   C   I and Ella

   D   he and Ella

2. Which pronoun would best complete Sentence 5?

   A   She

   B   They

   C   It

   D   Them

3. Which pronoun could replace the words *Sarah Goode* in Sentence 2?

   A   her

   B   she

   C   it

   D   them

4. Which of the following sentences has an incorrect pronoun?

   A   Sentence 2

   B   Sentence 3

   C   Sentence 4

   D   Sentence 5

5. Which pronoun could replace the second *families* in Sentence 3?

   A   we

   B   them

   C   they

   D   he

6. Which pronoun could replace the words *that invention* in Sentence 6?

   A   her

   B   it

   C   they

   D   us

▶ **Fill in each blank with a pronoun from the box. Not all of the pronouns will be used.**

me	her	it	him	I	she
he	they	we	us	them	

1. James thinks _____ would like to design video games.

2. Dion showed _____ a model of the toy he made.

3. My friend Noelle invented a game, and we played _____.

4. _____ told Rafiq that his idea would save people time.

5. Pia and _____ entered the competition together.

6. Damien is nervous, but his friends will be there with _____.

7. Raven asked Ron and _____ to help.

▶ **Rewrite each sentence. Replace the underlined word or words with a pronoun. Write *subject* or *object* to identify each kind of pronoun.**

8. <u>Fred</u> gave a report on <u>Tabitha Babbitt</u>.

_____

9. <u>Tabitha Babbitt</u> invented <u>the circular saw</u>.

_____

10. <u>Trey and Marie</u> told <u>Fred</u> the report was terrific.

_____

_____

Grammar Practice Book
© Harcourt • Grade 4

▶ **Write the possessive pronoun that could replace each group of words.**

	Before a Noun	Stand Alone
1. belonging to us	_____	_____
2. belonging to them	_____	_____
3. owned by the boy	_____	_____
4. belonging to me	_____	_____
5. belonging to you	_____	_____
6. the girl's	_____	_____

▶ **Rewrite each sentence, replacing the underlined word or words with a possessive pronoun.**

7. This is Danita's painting.

_____

8. The paper on the easel is Patrick's.

_____

9. "I think Danita's painting is the best," says Danita.

_____

10. Simon and Donna announce that the drawing is Simon's and Donna's.

_____

✎ **Try This**

If you were to draw a picture of yourself, what would it look like? Use possessive pronouns to write three sentences describing the picture. Include possessive pronouns that are used before nouns and possessive pronouns that stand alone.

Name _____

▶ **Choose the reflexive pronoun that can replace each
noun or pronoun.**

itself	yourself	herself	themselves
himself	myself	ourselves	

1. they _____

2. I _____

3. the chair _____

4. we _____

5. the girl _____

6. you _____

7. the boy _____

▶ **Rewrite the sentences. Choose the correct reflexive pronoun in parentheses ( ).**

8. Jerome wanted to paint (himself/themselves).

_____

9. We looked at (herself/ourselves) in the mirror.

_____

10. Would you like to draw (yourself/itself)?

_____

11. Did you think you could do it all by (yourselves/himself)?

_____

12. The woman said she would buy the paints (himself/herself).

_____

▶ **Read this part of a student's rough draft. Then answer the questions that follow.**

(1) Our teacher announced, "Today you will make a painting of your favorite thing." (2) She said the students could decide what to paint all by _____. (3) At first, many students just stared at the students' blank papers. (4) Then a boy named Fernando began painting birds on Fernando's paper. (5) Lucia began painting basketballs on hers. (6) Soon we were all enjoying ourselves!

1. Which is a reflexive pronoun?

    A   Our (Sentence 1)

    B   your (Sentence 1)

    C   hers (Sentence 5)

    D   ourselves (Sentence 6)

2. Which is the correct reflexive pronoun to fill in the blank in Sentence 2?

    A   themselves

    B   theirself

    C   themself

    D   themselfs

3. Which pronoun could replace the underlined words in Sentence 3?

    A   my

    B   their

    C   its

    D   our

4. Which sentence has a possessive pronoun that stands alone?

    A   Sentence 1

    B   Sentence 2

    C   Sentence 4

    D   Sentence 5

5. Which of these pronouns could replace the underlined word in Sentence 4?

    A   your

    B   her

    C   his

    D   its

6. Which is the antecedent for the pronoun *ourselves* in Sentence 6?

    A   boy

    B   Lucia

    C   basketballs

    D   we

Grammar Practice Book
© Harcourt • Grade 4

▶ **Write the pronoun in each sentence. Then write *P* if it is possessive or *R* if it is reflexive.**

1. The artists were pleased with their work. _____

2. The woman admired her paintings. _____

3. Juanita painted all of the portraits herself. _____

4. I gave my painting to a dear friend. _____

5. The sculpture was ours. _____

6. Did Maria put a price tag on yours? _____

7. William and Peter put the exhibit together themselves. _____

▶ **Rewrite each sentence. Correct any errors in the use of possessive or reflexive pronouns.**

8. Kyle said the illustration belonged to his.

   _____

9. That was mine picture!

   _____

10. Andrea put hers art supplies in the cabinet.

    _____

11. We helped ourself to more oil paints.

    _____

12. Joanie and Niall said they colored the poster himself.

    _____

▶ **Complete each sentence. Add an adjective of the type shown in parentheses ( ).**

1. The _____ art students packed their supplies. (what kind?)

2. Douglas collected _____ paintbrushes. (how many?)

3. Sophie put _____ tubes of paint in a box. (how many?)

4. The teacher led them to the _____ garden. (what kind?)

5. The students discussed the _____ landscape. (what kind?)

6. They sketched for _____ hours. (how many?)

7. _____ butterflies I was drawing flew away! (which ones?)

8. Elena sat on the _____ step. (which one?)

9. She had a _____ talent. (what kind?)

10. I thought her painting was _____! (what kind?)

▶ **Rewrite each sentence. Choose the correct articles from the parentheses ( ).**

11. (A/The) workers sat down in (a/the) chairs.

    _____

12. (An/The) group was meeting in (a/an) auditorium.

    _____

13. Reese suggested (a/an) idea for (a/an) website.

    _____

14. (A/The) bosses applauded her creativity.

    _____

15. It was (a/an) exciting meeting!

    _____

▶ **Underline the adjectives in each sentence. Then circle the noun each adjective describes.**

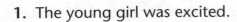

1. The young girl was excited.

2. The tall, thin poet stood on the stage.

3. The white spotlight was bright.

4. Many excited people sat in the audience.

5. The man opened his small, worn book.

6. In a warm, deep voice he read the poem.

7. The elderly woman enjoyed the wonderful performance.

▶ **Complete each sentence using two adjectives from the box. Use each adjective only once. Use correct punctuation.**

several	bright	colorful	pretty	ugly
exciting	young	many	big	dirty

8. The _____ lot was on the corner.

   _____

9. _____ children discussed how to clean it up.

   _____

10. A girl said they should paint a _____ mural.

    _____

11. One boy suggested planting _____ flowers.

    _____

12. The _____ project was a success!

    _____

▶ **Read this part of a student's rough draft. Then answer the questions that follow.**

> (1) Five big clowns got out of the tiny car. (2) They ran around in their big orange shoes. (3) The first clown made a loud noise, and two other clowns fell down. (4) A small child looked happy. (5) Suddenly the clowns threw their funny colorful hats into the air and ran away. (6) The circus tent became quiet again.

1. Which adjective in Sentence 3 tells *how many*?
   A first
   B loud
   C other
   D two

2. How many adjectives are in Sentence 1?
   A one
   B two
   C three
   D four

3. Which of these words is NOT an adjective?
   A Five (Sentence 1)
   B car (Sentence 1)
   C happy (Sentence 4)
   D funny (Sentence 5)

4. Which sentence is missing a comma between two adjectives?
   A Sentence 1
   B Sentence 3
   C Sentence 5
   D Sentence 6

5. What does the adjective *colorful* in Sentence 5 tell the reader?
   A how many
   B which one
   C which way
   D what kind

6. Which sentence has no articles?
   A Sentence 1
   B Sentence 2
   C Sentence 4
   D Sentence 6

▶ **Rewrite the letter. Add an adjective or adjectives to describe each underlined noun. Correct the articles when necessary.**

Dear Mom and Dad,

   I am having a **(1)** time at camp. After **(2)** days, I met **(3)** friends. We do **(4)** activities together.

   One **(5)** activity is arts and crafts class. I make **(6)** pots and paint them **(7)** colors. It takes **(8)** work, but I will be able to bring a **(9)** pot home to you!

   I am happy to be at **(16)** camp, and I feel lucky to have **(17)** parents. Please give my **(18)** dog a **(19)** hug from me.

                        Your **(20)** son,

                        Kyle

_____

_____

_____

_____

_____

_____

_____

_____

Name _____

▶ Write the form of the adjective used to compare people, places, or things.

	Compare One with One	**Compare One with More than One**
1. interesting	_____	_____
2. happy	_____	_____
3. great	_____	_____
4. hungry	_____	_____
5. amazing	_____	_____
6. cold	_____	_____

▶ Rewrite each sentence. Use the correct form of the adjective in parentheses.

7. The apple tree was the _____ of all the trees. (old)

_____

8. The apple is a _____ fruit than the pear. (popular)

_____

9. Leo said that strawberries are the _____ fruit of all. (delicious)

_____

10. The pears were the _____ pears he had ever eaten. (juicy)

_____

11. "This pear is _____ than that pear," stated the girl. (small)

_____

12. A grapefruit is _____ than an orange. (large)

_____

▶ Complete each sentence with a correct form of *good*.

1. Aunt Jackie's pumpkin pie is _____ than the one from the store.

2. Adding extra spices to the pie filling is a _____ idea.

3. Rene's apple pie is _____ than her last apple pie.

4. The competition is to find who makes the _____ peach preserves.

5. To grow the _____ flowers, you have to work hard.

6. Grandpa tells me that his garden is _____ than his neighbor's garden.

7. Luis thinks this book is _____ .

8. Of all of the stories I have read, this story is the _____ .

9. Do you think the ending of the story is _____ ?

10. That was the _____ of the three books.

▶ Complete each sentence with a correct form of *bad*.

11. That peach tasted _____ .

12. This year's harvest was _____ than last year's.

13. Aunt Lin said the berry crisp was the _____ she has ever tasted.

14. The old scarecrow looks _____ .

15. Jalinda said this year's lemons were the _____ she has ever seen.

16. John said that I was not a _____ gardener than he was.

17. I did not enjoy cooking because I was the _____ chef in my family.

18. The preserves were _____ , and I did not eat them.

19. The weather was _____ today than yesterday.

20. Yesterday I felt _____ because I ate too many crabapples.

▶ **Read this part of a student's rough draft. Then answer the questions that follow.**

> (1) Patty's Pies is the great bakery. (2) It has the <u>most best</u> cherry pie. (3) My friend Lee says that its apple pie is the <u>delicious</u> he has ever had. (4) The staff is <u>more nice</u> than the staff at the other local bakery. (5) You may notice that the decorations at Patty's Pies are _____ than those at the other bakery. (6) However, the pies are better at Patty's, and that is what counts!

1. Which is the correct way to write *great* when comparing three or more things (Sentence 1)?

   A greatest

   B more great

   C most great

   D correct as is

2. Which word or words should replace the underlined words in Sentence 2?

   A more good

   B best

   C more better

   D correct as is

3. Which word or words should replace the underlined word in Sentence 3?

   A deliciousest

   B more delicious

   C most delicious

   D correct as is

4. Which word or words should replace the underlined words in Sentence 4?

   A more nicer

   B most nice

   C nicer

   D nicest

5. Which adjective should fill in the blank in Sentence 5?

   A old

   B older

   C oldest

   D more older

6. Which sentence uses an adjective correctly to compare two things?

   A Sentence 2

   B Sentence 3

   C Sentence 5

   D Sentence 6

Name _____

▶ **Write the correct comparative form of the underlined adjective.**

1. Sean's basket of apples was <u>heavy</u> than Ollie's basket. _____

2. The tree in the front yard was <u>large</u> than the tree in the backyard.

   _____

3. Don said it was the <u>amazing</u> tree he had ever seen. _____

4. The field trip to the orchard was the <u>fun</u> I have had all week. _____

5. Of all the fruits, the cherry is the <u>good</u> fruit. _____

6. Don't you think that was the <u>interesting</u> field trip of all? _____

▶ **Rewrite each sentence. Correct the errors in the use of adjectives.**

7. Fran chose the colorful of the three cakes.

   _____

8. Was that menu most recent than the one we have at home?

   _____

9. Ana ate dinner more later than Tyrone.

   _____

10. That meal was the most better meal that Kate had ever eaten.

    _____

11. The pie tasted more bad than the cheesecake.

    _____

12. Mr. Young says the pastries are tastiest than the ones he made.

    _____

▶ **Read this part of a student's rough draft. Then answer the questions that follow.**

(1) This month our reading club had its anniversary party. (2) I baked the cake for the party myself. (3) My friends Raoul and Belinda helped me decorate it. (4) Raoul, Belinda, and I made the cake look like our club's first book. (5) Raoul did the writing on the cake by _____. (6) There were other desserts at the party, but the best one was ours!

1. Which is NOT a possessive pronoun?

   A   our (Sentence 1)

   B   its (Sentence 1)

   C   myself (Sentence 2)

   D   My (Sentence 3)

2. Which pronoun could replace the underlined words in Sentence 4?

   A   They

   B   We

   C   Us

   D   You

3. Which of the following sentences has a possessive pronoun that is not used before a noun?

   A   Sentence 2

   B   Sentence 4

   C   Sentence 5

   D   Sentence 6

4. Which is the antecedent for the pronoun *it* in Sentence 3?

   A   club

   B   party

   C   cake

   D   friends

5. Which reflexive pronoun could fill the blank in Sentence 5?

   A   yourself

   B   ourselves

   C   himself

   D   themselves

6. Which sentence has the most pronouns?

   A   Sentence 1

   B   Sentence 3

   C   Sentence 4

   D   Sentence 6

▶ **Read this part of a student's rough draft. Then answer the
questions that follow.**

> (1) The best pet Sandy ever owned was a small friendly pig named Gertrude.
> (2) She thought this pig was the most cute animal she had ever seen. (3) Sandy
> took good care of an adorable pig. (4) The most fun was taking Gertrude for walks
> down the street. (5) People gave Sandy <u>most cheerful</u> greetings than when she
> walked by herself. (6) "A pig is better than a dog for a pet!" said Sandy.

1. Which adjective from the passage
   tells *which one*?

   A best

   B this

   C good

   D fun

2. Which is the correct way to write
   cute when comparing more than
   two things in Sentence 2?

   A more cute

   B more cuter

   C cuter

   D cutest

3. Which is the correct word to replace
   the article in Sentence 3?

   A a

   B the

   C its

   D correct as is

4. Which word or words should
   replace the underlined words
   in Sentence 5?

   A cheerfuller

   B cheerfullest

   C more cheerful

   D correct as is

5. Which sentence is missing a comma
   between two adjectives?

   A Sentence 1

   B Sentence 2

   C Sentence 4

   D Sentence 5

6. Which noun does the adjective
   better describe in Sentence 6?

   A pig

   B dog

   C pet

   D Sandy

Name _____

▶ **Underline the verb in each sentence.**

1. We moved here last week.

2. I met a new friend today.

3. The librarian told me a story.

4. Long ago, a princess visited our town.

5. She brought her dog with her.

6. Many children read the book.

7. Older people remember the event.

▶ **Rewrite each sentence. Use a verb to complete each one.**

8. She _____ through the park.

   _____

9. My school day _____ at 8:30 A.M.

   _____

10. The large dog _____ to the child.

    _____

11. I _____ the family that lives upstairs.

    _____

12. The family _____ three children.

    _____

13. My father _____ the large box.

    _____

14. Do you _____ animals?

    _____

73

Grammar Practice Book

Name _____

▶ **Underline the main verb. Circle the helping verb.**

1. Toby's pet fish was swimming in the tank.

2. They have not purchased the fish bowl yet.

3. Toby's mother was walking to the pet store.

4. She will buy the largest fish bowl.

▶ **Rewrite each sentence. Use a helping verb and a form of the verb
in parentheses ( ).**

5. My dog (behave) inside the house.

   _____

6. A bear (scare) me, too.

   _____

7. The newspaper (publish) an article about the incident.

   _____

8. The woman (shake) her head.

   _____

9. You (go) outside to play.

   _____

10. The class (end) early today.

   _____

11. The schoolchildren (write) stories about their pets.

   _____

Grammar Practice Book
© Harcourt • Grade 4

▶ **Read this part of a student's rough draft. Then answer the questions that follow.**

> (1) My friend's dog escaped from the yard. (2) She had squeezed through the fence. (3) She ran down the street. (4) Soon she was panting hard. (5) Then we caught her. (6) We will definitely fix the hole in the fence!

1. Which has a helping verb?

   A Sentence 1

   B Sentence 2

   C Sentence 3

   D Sentence 5

2. Which is NOT a main verb in the passage?

   A escaped (Sentence 1)

   B had (Sentence 2)

   C caught (Sentence 5)

   D fix (Sentence 6)

3. Which are the main verbs in Sentences 2 and 6?

   A *squeezed* and *fix*

   B *had* and *fix*

   C *had* and *will*

   D *squeezed* and *definitely*

4. Which verb is NOT a helping verb in the passage?

   A had (Sentence 2)

   B was (Sentence 4)

   C caught (Sentence 5)

   D will (Sentence 6)

5. Which sentence does NOT have a helping verb?

   A Sentence 1

   B Sentence 2

   C Sentence 4

   D Sentence 6

6. Which sentence has another word between the helping verb and the main verb?

   A Sentence 1

   B Sentence 4

   C Sentence 5

   D Sentence 6

Name _____

▶ **For each sentence, write the main verb. Then write the helping verb.**

1. This dog food is made for larger dogs. _____

2. One bag of food can feed two adult Dalmatians.

   _____

3. I have developed a special formula for the food.

   _____

4. It could satisfy the hungriest of dogs! _____

5. This customer would like a sample. _____

6. I am buying two bags of this dog food. _____

▶ **Choose a helping verb from the box to complete each sentence. You may use a helping verb more than once or not at all.**

are	would	could	should
did	has	will	is

7. The store _____ staying open until 7:00 P.M.

8. Which flavor of ice cream _____ you like?

9. Katie _____ not make her choice yet.

10. _____ she ever eaten a banana split?

11. My family _____ bring potato salad to the picnic.

12. We _____ see huge storm clouds in the sky.

13. If it rains, the picnic _____ be canceled.

14. _____ we meeting at the park?

15. The weather forecast says that we _____ have sunny weather.

Name _____

▶ **Underline the verb in each sentence. Write** *action* **or**
linking **to tell what kind of verb it is.**

1. The family travels far from home. _____

2. We stay with my mother's sister. _____

3. They are very welcoming. _____

4. My father is a hard worker. _____

5. A union helps the workers. _____

6. Our new home seems nice. _____

7. My brothers and I speak Spanish. _____

▶ **Rewrite each sentence. Complete it with the kind of verb shown in
parentheses ( ).**

8. Marco _____ music on his guitar. (action)

_____

9. He _____ a talented musician. (linking)

_____

10. The children _____ anxious about traveling. (linking)

_____

11. My friends and I _____ to the park. (action)

_____

12. The whole family _____ good-bye. (action)

_____

 Try This ─────────────────────────────

Write four sentences about your family. Use two action verbs and two linking verbs.

Grammar Practice Book
© Harcourt • Grade 4

Name _____

▶ **Underline the action verbs. Circle the linking verbs.**

1. Claudio visits his grandparents in Mexico.

2. He feels excited about the trip.

3. Claudio's grandparents are happy about the visit, too.

4. Finally, the boy arrives.

5. A young girl named Juanita says hello.

6. She is about Claudio's age.

7. Claudio and Juanita play together.

▶ **Rewrite each sentence. Complete each one with a verb. Then write
whether you used an *action verb* or a *linking verb*.**

8. The young girl _____ in a diary.

   _____

9. She _____ worried.

   _____

10. The mother _____ the girl.

   _____

11. People _____ to a new country every day!

   _____

12. Soon, all of the relatives _____ together again.

   _____

► **Read this part of a student's rough draft. Then answer the questions that follow.**

> (1) Many people are on the bus. (2) The driver checks our tickets. (3) I feel nervous, but my brothers are excited. (4) We finally arrive at the bus station. (5) Our father is there! (6) He hugs and kisses all of us.

1. Which sentence has a linking verb?

  A Sentence 1

  B Sentence 2

  C Sentence 4

  D Sentence 6

2. Which is NOT an action verb?

  A checks (Sentence 2)

  B feel (Sentence 3)

  C arrive (Sentence 4)

  D hugs (Sentence 6)

3. Which describes the two verbs in Sentence 3?

  A *Feel* is linking and *are* is action.

  B *Feel* is action and *are* is linking.

  C They are both action verbs.

  D They are both linking verbs.

4. Which is NOT a linking verb?

  A are (Sentence 1)

  B feel (Sentence 3)

  C arrive (Sentence 4)

  D is (Sentence 5)

5. Which sentence has an action verb?

  A Sentence 1

  B Sentence 3

  C Sentence 4

  D Sentence 5

6. Which describes the two verbs in Sentence 6?

  A *Hugs* is linking and *kisses* is action.

  B *Hugs* is action and *kisses* is linking.

  C They are both action verbs.

  D They are both linking verbs.

Name _____

▶ **Write the main verb in each sentence. Then label each
one as *action* or *linking*.**

1. The car ride is long. _____

2. Raoul and Hector are tired from the trip. _____

3. That night, Mr. Diaz falls asleep immediately. _____

4. My mother and aunts cook breakfast. _____

5. Our home seems so far away. _____

6. I think about my friends there. _____

▶ **Add a verb to complete each sentence. Write *action* or *linking* to tell what kind of
verb you used.**

7. The city _____ noisy. _____

8. Lola _____ her bicycle. _____

9. A girl _____ across the yard. _____

10. She _____ friendly. _____

11. Hugo _____ used to the city sounds. _____

12. I _____ a quarter. _____

13. Lola _____ a tree in the park. _____

14. I _____ an ice-cream cone. _____

15. The ice cream _____ delicious. _____

Grammar Practice Book
© Harcourt • Grade 4

Name _____

Present-Tense
Verbs;
Subject-Verb
Agreement

Lesson 23

► **Circle the correct present-tense form of the verb in parentheses ( ).**

1. A cricket (jump, jumps) high in the air.

2. It (has, have) strong legs.

3. Do you (see, sees) many crickets in the city?

4. The big cat (look, looks) at the small insect.

5. The mice (hide, hides) behind the cupboard.

6. At the newsstand, workers (sell, sells) newspapers.

7. The subway (travel, travels) underground.

8. Mario (make, makes) a cage for his pet cricket.

9. My mother (think, thinks) crickets are noisy.

10. Some insects (chirp, chirps) loudly.

► **Rewrite each sentence. Use the correct present-tense form of the verb in parentheses ( ).**

11. Many birds (eat) insects.

_____

12. A cricket (rub) its wings together to make noise.

_____

13. An insect (have) three body sections.

_____

14. Bees, butterflies, and wasps (fly) around our garden.

_____

Grammar Practice Book
© Harcourt • Grade 4

Name _____

▶ **Write the form of the verb _be_ in each sentence. Then
write whether the subject is _singular_ or _plural_.**

1. They are at the theater already.

   _____

2. I am late for the show.

   _____

3. Her shoes are red.

   _____

4. The show is fantastic!

   _____

▶ **Rewrite each sentence with the correct present-tense form of the verb _be_.**

5. This neighborhood _____ near Times Square.

   _____

6. Many beautiful theaters _____ here.

   _____

7. I _____ amazed at the city's enormous size.

   _____

8. There _____ so much to see!

   _____

9. We _____ visiting the museum today.

   _____

10. I _____ looking forward to it.

   _____

82

▶ **Read this part of a student's rough draft. Then answer the questions that follow.**

> (1) Insects are an important part of Chinese culture. (2) Paintings and poems often _____ insects. (3) People keep insects for entertainment, too. (4) For example, a cricket may be kept as a pet. (5) A pet insect lives in a small cage. (6) Its song bring joy to its owner.

1. Which sentence has a present-tense form of the verb *be*?

   A Sentence 1

   B Sentence 3

   C Sentence 4

   D Sentence 5

2. Which has a plural form of a verb that should be in the singular form?

   A Sentence 1

   B Sentence 3

   C Sentence 5

   D Sentence 6

3. Which is a verb that agrees with its plural subject?

   A keep (Sentence 3)

   B makes (Sentence 4)

   C example (Sentence 4)

   D lives (Sentence 5)

4. Which verb could complete Sentence 2?

   A look

   B has

   C include

   D shows

5. Which sentence has a singular subject and a verb that agrees with it?

   A Sentence 1

   B Sentence 3

   C Sentence 5

   D Sentence 6

6. Which change, if any, should the student make to Sentence 6?

   A Change *Its* to *It*.

   B Change *bring* to *brings*.

   C Change *joy* to *joys*.

   D Make no change.

Name _____

▶ **Rewrite each sentence, adding a subject from the box.
Use each pronoun only once. Make sure that the subjects
and verbs agree.**

| I | You | She | It | They |

1. Can _____ read a book about zoo animals today?

   _____

2. _____ are all different kinds of animals.

   _____

3. _____ is a really great story.

   _____

4. _____ am not sure how it ends.

   _____

5. _____ keeps the book on her shelf.

   _____

▶ **Write the form of the verb *be* in each sentence. Then write whether the
subject is *singular* or *plural*.**

6. We are students in Mr. Stanley's writing class. _____

7. I am one of the best writers. _____

8. You are my favorite author. _____

9. This lesson is harder than last week's lesson. _____

10. Mr. Stanley tells us, "You are all very talented." _____

Grammar Practice Book
© Harcourt • Grade 4

▶ **Underline the complete verb in each sentence. Write**
past tense or *future tense* **to identify the tense of each verb.**

1. The photographer worked all day. _____

2. She used her best camera. _____

3. At sunset, the light faded away. _____

4. The photographs will be pretty. _____

5. She rowed the boat to shore. _____

6. The assistant viewed the images on the computer. _____

7. He will choose the best ones. _____

8. They shouted with happiness. _____

9. The editor at the newspaper will like your pictures. _____

10. He will pay for them. _____

▶ **Rewrite each sentence, using the correct form of the verb in parentheses ( ).**

11. Mango trees _____ in the orchard. (grow–past tense)

_____

12. The leaves _____ reddish. (look–past tense)

_____

13. Each mango fruit _____ a single seed. (contain–past tense)

_____

14. Mango flowers _____ in the spring or summer.
(appear–future tense)

_____

15. The fruit _____ about one pound. (weigh–future tense)

_____

Grammar Practice Book
© Harcourt • Grade 4

Name _____

▶ Complete the columns. Write the missing forms of each verb.

PRESENT TENSE	PAST TENSE	FUTURE TENSE
1. check	_____	_____
2. drag	_____	_____
3. _____	_____	will call
4. stop	_____	_____
5. _____	_____	will study
6. _____	rinsed	_____
7. _____	_____	will watch
8. _____	tried	_____
9. clean	_____	_____

▶ Rewrite the paragraph. Change the underlined present-tense verbs to their past-tense form.

Shawn (10) visits Florida and (11) learns about swamp life. The swamp (12) appears wet and wooded. Shawn (13) counts many different types of plants. He (14) likes the cypress trees best. Shawn and his sister (15) look for animals, such as turtles, otters, and herons.

_____

_____

_____

_____

▶ **Read this part of a student's rough draft. Then answer the questions that follow.**

> (1) We spotted two brown pelicans by the marina. (2) They live on the sandy beach. (3) The pelicans _____ fish. (4) They will use their bills and pouches to scoop up fish. (5) They build a nest on the ground. (6) Both the male bird and the female bird incubate the eggs.

1. Which sentence uses the past-tense form of a verb?
   A Sentence 1
   B Sentence 2
   C Sentence 4
   D Sentence 5

2. Which is a present-tense verb that could complete Sentence 3?
   A were
   B eat
   C caught
   D enjoyed

3. Which sentence uses a future-tense form of a verb?
   A Sentence 1
   B Sentence 2
   C Sentence 4
   D Sentence 5

4. Which change, if any, should be made in Sentence 5 to use a future-tense verb?
   A Change *build* to *builds*.
   B Change *build* to *will build*.
   C Change *build* to *built*.
   D Make no change.

5. Which change, if any, should be made in Sentence 6 to use a future-tense verb?
   A Change *incubate* to *will incubate*.
   B Change *incubate* to *incubates*.
   C Change *incubate* to *incubated*.
   D Make no change.

6. Which shows the correct present, past, and future tenses of a verb?
   A spot, spots, will spot
   B life, lived, will live
   C uses, used, will used
   D scoop, scooped, will scoop

▶ **Write the past-tense and future-tense forms of each present-tense verb.**

1. remark _____

2. surround _____

3. smile _____

4. bloom _____

5. trade _____

6. grin _____

7. hurry _____

▶ **Rewrite each sentence. Write the future-tense verbs in the past tense. Write the past-tense verbs in the future tense.**

8. The storm caused a lot of damage.

_____

9. We will check the yard after the storm.

_____

10. The heavy rain ruined my vegetable garden.

_____

11. Our neighbors' garage collapsed!

_____

12. They will report this to their insurance company.

_____

Grammar Practice Book
© Harcourt • Grade 4

▶ **Read this part of a student's rough draft. Then answer the questions that follow.**

(1) The volume of the radio was loud. (2) The announcer was yelling about a contest. (3) My friend Pedro had entered the contest. (4) We should listen for the winner. (5) Wow, Pedro has won a trip to China! (6) He is so excited!

1. Which sentence has a linking verb as its main verb?
   A   Sentence 1
   B   Sentence 2
   C   Sentence 4
   D   Sentence 5

2. Which is NOT a main verb in the passage?
   A   yelling (Sentence 2)
   B   entered (Sentence 3)
   C   should (Sentence 4)
   D   won (Sentence 5)

3. Which sentence does NOT have a helping verb?
   A   Sentence 2
   B   Sentence 3
   C   Sentence 5
   D   Sentence 6

4. Which is NOT a helping verb in the passage?
   A   was (Sentence 2)
   B   had (Sentence 3)
   C   should (Sentence 4)
   D   is (Sentence 6)

5. Which describes the verb *entered* in Sentence 3?
   A   helping and linking
   B   main and linking
   C   main and action
   D   helping and action

6. Which are the main verbs in Sentences 4 and 5?
   A   *listen* and *won*
   B   *listen* and *has*
   C   *should* and *won*
   D   *should* and *has*

▶ **Read this part of a student's rough draft. Then answer the questions that follow.**

> (1) Jamal is going to San Francisco. (2) He will ride a train from Arizona to California. (3) Jamal packed his bags. (4) Jamal and his sister walk to the train station. (5) The conductor shout, "All aboard!" (6) Jamal hugs his sister and <u>jumps</u> onto the train.

1. Which verb agrees in number with its plural subject?

  A is going (Sentence 1)

  B will ride (Sentence 2)

  C walk (Sentence 4)

  D hugs (Sentence 5)

2. Which sentence has a future-tense verb?

  A Sentence 1

  B Sentence 2

  C Sentence 3

  D Sentence 6

3. Which sentence has a verb that does not agree with its singular subject?

  A Sentence 1

  B Sentence 3

  C Sentence 4

  D Sentence 5

4. Which describes the verb *hugs* in Sentence 6?

  A past-tense

  B future-tense

  C present-tense

  D plural

5. Which is the past-tense form of the underlined verb in Sentence 6?

  A jumped

  B jump

  C will jump

  D jumping

6. Which sentence has a past-tense verb?

  A Sentence 1

  B Sentence 2

  C Sentence 3

  D Sentence 6

Name _____

▶ **Write the past-tense form for each present-tense verb.**

1. go _____

2. begin _____

3. wear _____

4. throw _____

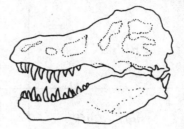

▶ **Rewrite each sentence. Use the correct past-tense form of the verb in parentheses ( ).**

5. Ancient people _____ the huge bones belonged to giants. (think)

_____

6. They _____ wrong. (be)

_____

7. The scientist _____ the skull in the museum's basement. (find)

_____

8. He _____ the answer to the student's question. (know)

_____

9. Hank's model of a dinosaur skeleton _____. (break)

_____

10. We _____ him a new model. (give)

_____

Grammar Practice Book
© Harcourt • Grade 4

Name _____

▶ **Complete the chart with the correct forms of each verb.**

VERB	PRESENT	PAST	PAST WITH HELPING VERBS (have, has, had)
1. wear	wear, wears	_____	_____
2. go	go, goes	_____	_____
3. know	know, knows	_____	_____
4. break	break, breaks	_____	_____
5. begin	begin, begins	_____	_____
6. throw	throw, throws	_____	_____
7. be	am, is, are	_____	_____
8. choose	choose, chooses	_____	_____
9. draw	draw, draws	_____	_____
10. eat	eat, eats	_____	_____

▶ **Write this present-tense paragraph in the past tense.**

Sama **(11)** is a good reader. Over the summer, she **(12)** goes to the library every day. Sama **(13)** chooses a new book each time. Then she **(14)** begins to read. By the end of the summer, she **(15)** knows a lot about many different things.

_____

_____

_____

_____

Grammar Practice Book
© Harcourt • Grade 4

▶ **Read this part of a student's rough draft. Then answer the questions that follow.**

> (1) We went to the Natural History Museum yesterday. (2) The tour of the dinosaur exhibit was two hours long. (3) The museum guide suggested that we wear comfortable shoes. (4) Instead, Arnie wore his brand-new boots. (5) He had <u>thought</u> it was a good idea. (6) After just 15 minutes, Arnie knew he had made a mistake!

1. Which verb from the passage is the past-tense form of the verb *go*?

    A went (Sentence 1)

    B was (Sentence 2)

    C wear (Sentence 3)

    D wore (Sentence 4)

2. Which sentence has one verb in the present tense and one in the past tense?

    A Sentence 2

    B Sentence 3

    C Sentence 4

    D Sentence 5

3. Which two sentences have a helping verb?

    A Sentences 2 and 3

    B Sentences 3 and 4

    C Sentences 4 and 5

    D Sentences 5 and 6

4. Which two sentences do NOT include a past-tense form of the verb *be*?

    A Sentences 1 and 2

    B Sentences 3 and 4

    C Sentences 4 and 5

    D Sentences 5 and 6

5. Which verb is the past-tense form of the verb *be*?

    A went (Sentence 1)

    B was (Sentence 2)

    C wear (Sentence 3)

    D wore (Sentence 4)

6. The underlined verb in Sentence 4 is the past-tense form of which verb?

    A thrill

    B throw

    C think

    D theft

Name _____

▶ **Rewrite the underlined verbs in the past tense.**

1. Writing stories about dinosaurs is Jane's favorite pastime. _____

2. She begins with a description of the dinosaur. _____

3. Jane thinks of its habitat. _____

4. Then she writes about events from her imagination. _____

5. When she makes a mistake, she throws the page away. _____

6. The stories are always great! _____

7. Jane knows so much about these animals. _____

▶ **Write a sentence to answer each question. Use the past-tense form of the verb you see in the question.**

8. When did you go to bed last night?

   _____

9. What kind of shoes did you wear yesterday?

   _____

10. When did you begin your homework?

   _____

11. What did you see on your way to school today?

   _____

12. What did you think of the book?

   _____

Name _____

▶ **Write the contraction for each word pair.**

1. she is _____

2. is not _____

3. they have _____

4. does not _____

5. will not _____

6. should not _____

7. you are _____

8. I am _____

9. we had _____

10. it is _____

▶ **Label each underlined word as a *contraction* or a *possessive pronoun*.**

11. We're tired from walking so far. _____

12. The door wouldn't close. _____

13. Its hinge is broken. _____

14. After lunch, they weren't tired anymore. _____

15. The hikers put on their backpacks. _____

16. It's a long way to the bottom of the canyon! _____

17. Your face looks sunburned. _____

18. I've put on sunscreen and a hat. _____

19. I think they're resting. _____

20. Imagine you're already at the top of the hill. _____

95

► Circle the word in parentheses ( ) that correctly completes the sentence.

1. (It's, Its) time to stop for water.

2. (They're, Their) shoes are dry and dusty.

3. I count (four, for) coyotes.

4. The pack mules (no, know) which trail to follow.

5. (Your, You're) taking some great pictures.

6. They plan to hike tomorrow, (to, too).

► Rewrite each sentence. Use the correct word from the box to complete it.

new	knew	heard	herd	right	write

7. This sleeping bag is _____.

_____

8. I _____ Dora yell with excitement.

_____

9. We see a _____ of buffalo!

_____

10. _____ me a postcard when you have time.

_____

11. They _____ the way to the campsite.

_____

12. Are you sure Dora is _____?

_____

Grammar Practice Book

▶ **Read this part of a student's rough draft. Then answer the questions that follow.**

> (1) In two days I'm visiting Yosemite National Park with my cousins. (2) They have been to the park before, but I haven't. (3) My cousins say they're favorite part of the trip is seeing all of the stars at night. (4) I can't wait too see the stars. (5) I know its going to be fantastic!

1. Which word pair does the contraction *I'm* in Sentence 1 stand for?

   A   I may

   B   I am

   C   I might

   D   I have

2. Which is the contraction for the underlined words in Sentence 2?

   A   They've

   B   The've

   C   They'd

   D   They're

3. Which word pair does the contraction *haven't* in Sentence 2 stand for?

   A   have nothing

   B   have no

   C   have not

   D   have never

4. Which sentence incorrectly uses a contraction where there should be a possessive pronoun?

   A   Sentence 1

   B   Sentence 2

   C   Sentence 3

   D   Sentence 5

5. Which sentence incorrectly uses a possessive pronoun where there should be a contraction?

   A   Sentence 2

   B   Sentence 3

   C   Sentence 4

   D   Sentence 5

6. In which sentence is one of the words *two*, *too*, or *to* used incorrectly?

   A   Sentence 1

   B   Sentence 2

   C   Sentence 4

   D   Sentence 5

▶ **Write the contraction for each word pair.**

1. can not _____

2. they had _____

3. do not _____

4. you have _____

5. we have _____

6. are not _____

7. were not _____

▶ **Write whether the underlined word is *correct* or *incorrect*. If the word is incorrect, write the correct one.**

8. Their are many wonderful parks in the United States. _____

9. I haven't been too them all. _____

10. If you've seen the Grand Canyon, you're lucky. _____

11. My sister has heard that it is more than 275 miles long.

    _____

12. I've read it is about won mile deep! _____

13. Its a five-hour trip to the deepest part of the canyon. _____

14. Ollie's parents showed us their photographs of the Grand Canyon.

    _____

15. I no I want to go there some day. _____

Name _____

▶ **Circle the adverb. Then write whether the adverb tells**
where, when, **or** *how.*

1. Paul Bunyan worked hard to clear the land. _____

2. Paul Bunyan walked everywhere. _____

3. Paul fell in love with Carrie immediately. _____

4. Later, they got married. _____

5. My mother sings happily. _____

6. Sometimes I join in the song. _____

7. Niagara Falls is over there. _____

8. Today we are walking in Bryce Canyon. _____

▶ **Rewrite each sentence. Use the correct form of the adverb in parentheses ( ).**

9. The Bunyan children grow _____ than the neighbor's children. (quick)

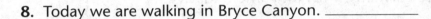

_____

10. The girl _____ wrestled a puma. (brave)

_____

11. The family travels _____. (wide)

_____

12. They enjoy their trips _____. (great)

_____

🖊 **Try This**

Choose one adverb of each type, for example *upstairs, frequently,* and *softly.* Then use each adverb in a sentence that compares more than two actions.

99

Grammar Practice Book
© Harcourt • Grade 4

▶ **Underline each verb, and circle the adverb that describes it. Then write the negative from each sentence.**

1. Nobody chops down trees better than Paul Bunyan. _____

2. It was not difficult for him to cut trees more quickly than other loggers.

   _____

3. No ox worked harder than Babe. _____

4. No place looks more beautiful than Big Sur._____

5. I've never met anyone who could sing more loudly than Sue. _____

▶ **Rewrite each sentence correctly, with only one negative.**

6. He had never seen no big mountains before.

   _____

7. There is not nothing wrong with being a lumberjack.

   _____

8. The other loggers were not never as fast as Paul.

   _____

9. Paul hadn't seen nothing like Babe before.

   _____

10. He couldn't imagine no finer ox.

   _____

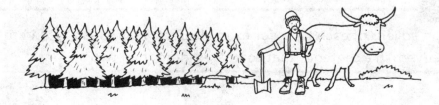

Grammar Practice Book
© Harcourt • Grade 4

▶ **Read this part of a student's rough draft. Then answer the questions that follow.**

> (1) Of all the famous characters in folktales, Babe the Blue Ox worked hardest. (2) No animal was never as strong as Babe. (3) Babe labored more than Paul Bunyan did! (4) I happily read any stories about Paul and Babe. (5) I thought they were the best stories of all. (6) I will write about the story tomorrow.

1. Which of the following is NOT an adverb in the passage?

   A hardest (Sentence 1)

   B strong (Sentence 2)

   C more (Sentence 3)

   D happily (Sentence 4)

2. Which are being compared in Sentence 1?

   A Babe and folktales

   B Babe and famous characters

   C famous characters and folktales

   D Babe and the Blue Ox

3. Which is NOT described by an adverb?

   A worked (Sentence 1)

   B labored (Sentence 3)

   C read (Sentence 4)

   D thought (Sentence 5)

4. Which sentence has a double negative?

   A Sentence 1

   B Sentence 2

   C Sentence 3

   D Sentence 5

5. Which sentence compares just two actions?

   A Sentence 1

   B Sentence 3

   C Sentence 4

   D Sentence 5

6. Which is an adverb that tells *when*?

   A hardest (Sentence 1)

   B happily (Sentence 4)

   C best (Sentence 5)

   D tomorrow (Sentence 6)

Name _____

▶ **Fill in the chart with the correct forms of each adverb.**

ADVERB	COMPARING TWO ACTIONS	COMPARING MORE THAN TWO ACTIONS
1. quietly	_____	_____
2. high	_____	_____
3. frequently	_____	_____
4. well	_____	_____
5. carefully	_____	_____
6. early	_____	_____

▶ **Rewrite the sentences. Use adverbs from the chart above. Correct all double negatives.**

7. I read books _____ than Kate does.

_____

8. Paul Bunyan jumps the _____ of all.

_____

9. She plays _____ than her younger sister does.

_____

10. Paul doesn't think no animal works _____ than Babe.

_____

▶ **Complete each sentence by adding a comma, colon, or hyphen. Write *comma, colon,* or *hyphen* to identify the punctuation mark you added.**

1. I once visited Anchorage _____ Alaska. _____

2. This is what I took _____ a camera, my suitcase, and a travel book. _____

3. My uncle, who is twenty _____ two, also came. _____

4. One day, we took the train to Fairbanks _____ Alaska. _____

5. I ate chocolate _____ covered peanuts on the train. _____

6. I saw these animals from the train _____ a moose, a bear, and a fox. _____

7. The train arrived in the Fairbanks station at 7 _____ 30 P.M. _____

8. My trip ended on August 20 _____ 2006. _____

▶ **Rewrite each sentence. Correctly write each title.**

9. John Muir wrote a book called The Story of My Boyhood and Youth.

_____

10. Alaska's Flag is the title of the state song.

_____

11. My mom thinks the newspaper USA Today is the best newspaper.

_____

12. Have you seen the movie 101 Dalmatians?

_____

13. A young orphan takes in a stray dog in the play Annie.

_____

14. Charlotte's Web is my favorite book.

_____

103

▶ **If the use of quotation marks is correct, write** *correct***. If the use of quotation marks is incorrect, write** *incorrect***.**

1. "What do you know about Alaska? asked Philip." _____

2. "I know it became the forty-ninth state in 1959," answered Drea.

   _____

3. Samuel said, "Isn't Alaska the largest state? _____

4. It's twice the size of Texas! exclaimed Raoul. _____

5. The largest city is Anchorage, "said Anna." _____

▶ **Rewrite each sentence. Add quotation marks and commas where they are needed.**

6. Have you heard of Mt. McKinley? asked Yetta.

   _____

7. It is the highest point in North America said Marvin.

   _____

8. Win said, Alaska became a state on January 3 1959.

   _____

9. The state flower is the forget-me-not, announced Jay.

   _____

10. Alaska has a lot of oil said Patik.

    _____

11. Debbie said, Oil is an important natural resource.

    _____

12. You can travel to Juneau, Alaska, only by boat or by plane, said Zora.

    _____

104

▶ **Read this part of a student's rough draft. Then answer the questions that follow.**

> (1) "On October 5 2008, there will be a performance at Anchorage Elementary School, said Mr. Pearson, the principal. (2) Tell us what the fourth-grade students will perform, said Mr. Clark. (3) "The students will perform a scene from the play Our Great State" answered Mr. Pearson. (4) "What time does the play start?" asked Ms. Kert. (5) "The play starts at 800 P.M. said the principal."

1. Which sentence is NOT missing a comma?
   A   Sentence 1
   B   Sentence 2
   C   Sentence 3
   D   Sentence 5

2. Which sentence is missing a colon?
   A   Sentence 1
   B   Sentence 2
   C   Sentence 4
   D   Sentence 5

3. Which of the following should be underlined?
   A   Anchorage Elementary School (Sentence 1)
   B   Principal Pearson (Sentence 1)
   C   Our Great State (Sentence 3)
   D   Ms. Kert (Sentence 4)

4. Which sentence has no errors?
   A   Sentence 1
   B   Sentence 3
   C   Sentence 4
   D   Sentence 5

5. Where should quotation marks be added in Sentence 2?
   A   before *Tell* and after *perform,*
   B   before *Tell* and after *Clark.*
   C   before *Tell*
   D   after *Clark.*

6. Which is the name of the punctuation mark between the words *fourth* and *grade* in Sentence 2?
   A   comma
   B   quotation mark
   C   hyphen
   D   colon

▶ **Rewrite each sentence. Correct any mistakes in punctuation.**

1. The book Old Yeller is about a dog and a boy.

   _____

2. The setting of the story is Salt Lick Texas.

   _____

3. I like that story a lot says Daisy.

   _____

4. Ernesto says The movie Lassie is better.

   _____

5. I take three things to the park my ball my bat and my jacket.

   _____

6. What are you reading asks Fletcher.

   _____

7. He is reading The Mouse and the Motorcycle.

   _____

8. Edie sings This Land Is Your Land with me.

   _____

9. Kaia's mother is thirty seven years old.

   _____

10. James says My dog is the best dog in the world!

    _____

▶ **Read this part of a student's rough draft. Then answer the questions that follow.**

(1) Last year Grandma and I moved to a new town. (2) We had thought that we would not know anyone there, but we did! (3) The Pattersons, friends from our old neighborhood, brought us brownies when we moved in. (4) They're house was next door. (5) Patty Patterson said that we will go to the same school. (6) Its so nice to have friends!

1. Which sentence has helping verbs?

   A Sentence 1

   B Sentence 2

   C Sentence 3

   D Sentence 6

2. Which is the contraction for the word pair *would not* in Sentence 2?

   A wouldn't

   B won't

   C weren't

   D wasn't

3. Of which verb is *brought* (Sentence 3) the past-tense form?

   A begin

   B be

   C bring

   D bristle

4. Which sentence incorrectly uses a possessive pronoun where there should be a contraction?

   A Sentence 3

   B Sentence 4

   C Sentence 5

   D Sentence 6

5. Which sentence incorrectly uses a contraction where there should be a possessive pronoun?

   A Sentence 2

   B Sentence 4

   C Sentence 5

   D Sentence 6

6. Which verb is the past-tense form of the verb *think*?

   A thought (Sentence 2)

   B brought (Sentence 3)

   C was (Sentence 4)

   D said (Sentence 5)

Grammar Practice Book
© Harcourt • Grade 4

▶ **Read this part of a student's rough draft. Then answer the questions that follow.**

(1) First prize for the Book Report Fair goes to Shelly King announced Mr. Langley. (2) "Her report on Shipwreck at the Bottom of the World was the best of all, said Ms. Winston. (3) I think I worked harder than Shelly did," said Evan. (4) "Come quickly to get your ribbon, Shelly!" called out Mr. Langley. (5) Shelly was not nowhere to be found. (6) "Can I have the prize, then?" Evan asked hopefully.

1. Which sentence is missing a comma?
   A   Sentence 1
   B   Sentence 2
   C   Sentence 3
   D   Sentence 5

2. Which sentence has a double negative?
   A   Sentence 1
   B   Sentence 2
   C   Sentence 3
   D   Sentence 5

3. Which is NOT an adverb?
   A   first (Sentence 1)
   B   harder (Sentence 3)
   C   quickly (Sentence 4)
   D   hopefully (Sentence 6)

4. Which sentence is NOT missing one or more quotation marks?
   A   Sentence 1
   B   Sentence 2
   C   Sentence 3
   D   Sentence 4

5. Which should be underlined?
   A   Book Report Fair (Sentence 1)
   B   Shelly King (Sentence 1)
   C   Shipwreck at the Bottom of the World (Sentence 2)
   D   Mr. Langley (Sentence 4)

6. Which sentence compares two actions?
   A   Sentence 1
   B   Sentence 2
   C   Sentence 3
   D   Sentence 4

INDEX

A

Abbreviations, 38–40, 53
Action verbs, 77–80
Adjectives, 63–66, 72
    comparing with, 67–70, 72
Adverbs, 99–102, 108
    comparing with, 101–102, 108
Antecedents
    agreement with pronouns, 49–52,
        54, 61, 71
Apostrophes
    in contractions, 95, 97–98, 107
    in possessive nouns, 45–48
Articles, 63, 65–66, 72

B

Be (verb), 74, 76, 82–84, 93

C

Capitalization
    of proper nouns, 39, 53
    of sentences, 1–4
    of titles, 40, 103, 105–106, 108
Clauses
    dependent, 31, 33–34, 36
    independent, 31, 33–34
Commas, 103–106, 108
    between adjectives, 65, 72
    in complex sentences, 32–34
    in compound sentences, 24–26
    in compound subjects and predicates,
        20–22

Common nouns, 37, 39–40
Complete predicates, 13–16, 18
Complete sentences, 1, 3
Complete subjects, 13–16, 18
Complex sentences, 32–34, 36
Compound predicates, 19–22, 26
Compound sentences, 23–26, 32, 35
Compound subjects, 19–22, 26, 35
Conjunctions, 20, 23–26
Contractions, 95, 97–98, 107

D

Declarative sentences, 1–4, 17
Dependent clauses, 31, 33–34, 36

E

End marks, 1–8, 17
Exclamatory sentences, 5–8, 17

F

Future-tense verbs, 85–88, 90

H

Helping verbs, 74–76, 89, 93, 107

I

Imperative sentences, 5–8, 17
Independent clauses, 31, 33–34
Interjections, 6–8
Interrogative sentences, 1–4, 17
Irregular verbs, 91–94, 107

L

Linking verbs, 77–80, 89

M

Main and helping verbs, 73–76, 80, 89, 93, 107

Mechanics
See Capitalization; Punctuation

N

Negatives, 100–102, 108

Nouns
common, 37, 39–40
plural possessive, 45–48, 54
possessive, 45–48, 54
proper, 37, 39–40, 53
singular and plural, 41–44, 46–48, 53–54

O

Object pronouns, 55–58

P

Past-tense verbs, 85–88, 90–94, 107

Possessive nouns, 45–48, 54

Possessive pronouns, 59, 61–62, 71, 95, 97, 107

Predicates, 9–12
complete, 13–16, 18
compound, 19–22, 26
simple, 13–16, 18, 21, 35

Prepositional phrases, 27–30, 36

Prepositions, 27–30, 36

Present-tense verbs, 81–83, 86, 90, 93

Pronouns, 49–52, 54, 71
antecedents of, 49–52, 54, 61, 71
plural possessive, 59, 61–62, 71, 95, 97, 107
possessive, 59, 61–62, 71, 95, 97, 107
reflexive, 60–62, 71
subject and object, 55–58

Proper nouns, 37, 39–40, 53

Punctuation
apostrophes in contractions, 95, 97–98, 107
apostrophes in possessive nouns, 45–48
colons, 103, 105–106
commas, 103–106, 108
end marks, 1–8, 17
quotation marks, 104–106, 108
titles, 40, 103, 105–106, 108

Q

Quotation marks, 104–106, 108

R

Reflexive pronouns, 60–62, 71

Run-on sentences, 24–25, 35

S

Sentences
capitalization of, 1–4
complex, 32–34, 36
compound, 23–26, 32, 35
run-on, 24–25, 35
simple, 23, 32–33, 35

Grammar Practice Book
© Harcourt • Grade 4